POP SMOKE

POP SMOKE

A MEMOIR OF FAMILY AND COURAGE

T. S. ARTHER

PALMETTO
PUBLISHING
Charleston, SC
www.PalmettoPublishing.com

Pop Smoke
Copyright © 2023 by T. S. Arther

First Edition

Hardcover ISBN: 979-8-8229-2438-3
Paperback ISBN: 979-8-8229-2439-0

I believe when you're stuck in one spot for too long it's best to throw a grenade where you stand, and jump…and pray – Robyn Davidson.

TABLE OF CONTENTS

AUTHOR'S NOTE

When I didn't know what else to do, I turned to the essence of my profession—human resources, customer service, and putting everyone else's needs before my own—to cope with taking up a space where I never felt as if I belonged. I soon realized that my field of knowledge and expertise were not enough for such a significant task. I needed something cogent, something realistic and measurable, and something that would keep me tethered to the essence of life like handcuffs. As I took a turn down memory lane in my life, the many lessons that I learned have prepared me to navigate the life I now choose for myself. I realized that writing had been a constant battle buddy of mine, never leaving my heart or my side, a craft I can share, give all of me, and not feel lethargic or empty.

I have gone through extensive research during the pandemic finding lost loved ones and trying to force-piece an old puzzle together to represent a new flawless picture. However, nothing in life is perfect. Some names in this book have been changed because they have either been long lost, forgotten or played such a minor but memorable part in my experience. Either way, it doesn't take from the validity of my story. And to those who may question why even name-drop at all I would say, if you didn't want to be a character in someone else's story then you should have behaved better. I've written my peace.

PROLOGUE

1991. I grew up in the heart and soul of Milwaukee in a neighborhood, strewn with bald patches amidst the overgrown grass and heavy graffiti on old, industrialized buildings—all vacant when the jobs were outsourced. On a map, you could triangulate with a red Sharpie all the places my family moved to within the heart of the city, from Capital Drive to Burleigh Street to Fondulac Avenue. Most of our houses had chain-linked fences that had been robbed of their front gates. The mysterious metal bandits compiled scrap metal for a few bucks, leaving behind a gap and a cold trail in front of homes. Within each neighborhood, you'd see the missing puzzle pieces vanish, like ghosts, which makes you wonder why you can't have nice shit. The missing front gates must only happen in the rougher neighborhoods.

Life looked a lot different from what I saw was shown on TV. For starters, you didn't get orchestral music during life's egregious moments. You didn't hear when Mama staggered in drunkenly late in the hour from taverns while my siblings and I were tucked in bed. But you know, at least there was some type of music playing in that scenario, maybe a little Run DMC, LL Cool J, or Public Enemy.

Nowadays, a lot of families eat dinner in separate rooms at separate times, in front of separate televisions—whereas my TV family sat down at the same large table and shared a meal together that always reminded me of Thanksgiving Day. The families on TV yap and laugh, their gums kiss, and they barely touch anything on their fine china. Sometimes I anxiously waited to hear the clacking of their shiny silver forks—that never meet their mouths—against their nice plates, to waste.

In the summer months in my neighborhood, the outdoors felt hot as fish grease. The air smelled like freshly fried food and high cholesterol, *home sweet home*. But despite the feel of the neighborhood, the corner bodegas carried the best hot hog head cheese and liver cheese that we loved to stack on saltine crackers. Don't knock it 'til you try it. With those families on TV, you can tell they had money. They could afford to waste food. Mama would always spout absurdly, "Children over in Africa are starving!"

I saw Dad get up and go to work every single day. He never missed work. Dad served as a fast-food manager back then. Extremely ambitious, he managed both a McDonald's and a Burger King. He smoked a lot of cigarettes, too. Dad also had a side hustle policing up aluminum cans left out on the streets with his homeboys, who I called the "clean-up crew." They earned extra cash for cigarettes, beer, and gas for a Cadillac Dad drove smoothly with a gangster's lean.

Mama had no job, but she spent heaps of time volunteering at the various elementary schools, like the ones my siblings and I attended when we did not want her there—when we weren't moving for the umpteenth time because we couldn't make ends meet. Seeing Mama in the halls of our school every day, I knew I couldn't get into any trouble, so I sat like a perfect angel, with my hands folded on top of my desk, feeling all those eyes piercing me as she entered and exited my classroom at will. By the time I entered the fifth grade, I had already gone to four schools and couldn't maintain a friendship to save my life. After years of volunteering, Mama landed herself a permanent position at Siefert Elementary School as a teacher's aide.

When Dad and Mama separated for the final time, Mama went out looking for love all in temporary places. Sometimes love was six feet tall, bald, and ugly wearing Coke bottle glasses— someone she met at the bar—turning up Rum and Coke.

Not only did I love my dad, but I also admired him. I think, deep down, Mama resented the amount of adoration I had for Dad, and it showed in the way that she spoke and maneuvered her body. Sometimes, I felt the backlash from my favoring one parent over the other.

I thought what I really needed was a family unit like the Huxtables. I learned to internalize what I knew to be Black sorrows, Black struggles, and Black pains, outwardly looking for Black joy. The Huxtables represented both strong family values and education—characteristics that I grew to admire, characteristics Mama's family didn't have. Barriers were broken in the moments when I never saw myself equated with greatness because the magazines and television not only told me so subliminally, but they also showed me who I was not. And sometimes the words of Dad, "You are the most beautiful brown girl in the whole wide world," weren't enough even though I still knew at the same time that was the great-est affirmation I could ask for growing up because I real-ized at that moment that Black fathers matter, too. I also knew this because, throughout high school, I shared Dad with my friends who weren't as close to their own or who never knew them. Our house became the hang-out spot af-ter school hours or on the weekends. Some days it bothered me to share Dad with others. But then I thought about the joy of seeing others have joy in the presence of Dad. Not too many people know joy; they only know pleasure, temporary pleasing. Spreading joy was Dad's superpower.

Now, insomnia greets me when my head meets my pillow, and I mourn the loss of my gentle giant, my Black Superman—I call him Daddy. In my eyes, Dad always seemed ten feet tall. He always taught me life's most valu-able lessons, and how to be a better person. But after his death, life got challenging, and life got complicated because grieving is unmeasurable and unpredictable. Everyone has an expiration date, but there are no words to express every level of emotion I would soon begin to feel. People I knew and even loved offered pity, but many of them I never heard from again. And others wanted to know how to move on from loss, how to move on from the pain that you feel inside. They wanted to know how I am so strong through all of this because they only see what is presented outwardly when in-ternally I'm withering away. I'm learning to live without the joy I'm used to having in my life, a life without him, a life without Superman.

But here I am. I am laying out all my truths, my ex-periences, my losses, my battle—revealing things I've never shared aloud with anyone other than the lady sitting in front of me every other Tuesday, looking at me, brown like me, gawking at me. She has these blank expressions holding a pen and her pad on her lap, giving me textbook advice and even homework for application.

If I had the opportunity to go back and chat with the younger me, I've often thought about what I might say. I do not know what I would tell the younger, more vulnerable me. But I think about the moments hanging out on the couch with Dad watching horror movies, preferably zombies ripping flesh from unruly teenagers. I remember how Dad would say, "They shouldn't have split up." Or, how he would say, "They gone mess around and write a check that they ass can't cash!" His finger pointed at the television screen. "They should have had a better plan." And other times, he'd shout, "Run, bitch, run!" Because when shit got real, they stumble and fall. All four lines are good advice for a girl like me, I suppose.

Dad's apartment had cable; Mama's place only had a few channels. Dad was fun, but Mama was not. At least with Dad, I had a sense of family values and tradition. Mama was an orphan. The emotional balance of her raising three children seemed cold. There were no hugs and kisses, birthday wishes, and no extra gifts waiting under the Christmas tree.

And what I didn't get from Mama, I looked forward to receiving from Grandma Lizz before she also gained her wings. I will miss the times of having a small cup of coffee with my paternal grandma before she would say something weird. "Coffee gives you wrinkles," she'd warn. She hoped I would not make caffeine such a bad habit at an early age. However, I would not care about facial lines and how they'd dissect one another because I was nine, and then I had all the time in the world. When you are nine, it's like you're invincible, and I wanted to be everything from Miss America, a flight attendant, to a chance at being the first woman president.

Furthermore, I wanted to emulate Grandma Lizz reading the morning newspaper and sitting next to Grandpa Zeke Sr., who was the love of her life. But all I have are fading memories of people who taught me more than I would ever learn on my own. I still have my morning cups of coffee along with my local *Wavy News*. At forty, I smile at the thought of being invincible. I smile at the thought of loving someone so important in my life. "It's not about having time; it's about making time" is one of my favorite quotes that I live by daily. I chose this way of living after watching Dad slowly die. I learned that time well spent is not only precious but valuable.

It's amazing how long he triumphed under any circumstance. Amazingly, he was chosen as my dad. So, I hold close to my heart a photo of the three of us. A photo of two teenagers with a baby. And it is quite clear who my protector would always be.

Dad is gripping what looks like a tiny pink sack. A baby tucked away cradled in his arms like a football. Mama's wild, bushy hair leans heavily against the wind. She's wearing her graphic t-shirt, and flare-legged jeans, standing next to a tall, hunk of a man. He's wearing a retro Minnesota Twins baseball t-shirt. I cannot believe the tiny baby inside Dad's arms is really me. I can still feel his heartbeat next to mine. I can still feel the joy of his smile shining down on me. I remember all the stories he told me as I grew older of the times my small body fit perfectly inside his coat during the winter months in Wisconsin. I was so tiny then, about six pounds. He sang to me. I miss his voice. I could still hear the words, "Dad is great, great, great," echoing from the back of my mind. The man in the photo standing next to Mama has the stance of Superman. He comforts me, shielding me from chilly Midwestern temperatures. He tells me over and over that I am the most beautiful brown girl in his whole-wide world. I am his bundle of joy delicately wrapped in pretty pastel pinks, topped with a bow. I am held in the arms of my one true king. I am packaged like a gift my parents waited a long nine months to receive.

The strength of Dad's arm hung around Mama's shoulders, as he pulled her body tightly into his. Both of my parents looked so proud together, showing me off to their imperfect little world. The three of us are outside of Dad's tan Cadillac, parked outside of the foster home where Mama used to live—a life Mama had that I would hardly ever know.

I can still smell Dad's scent of Old Spice coming from the blue-sleeved Minnesota baseball T-shirt he kept for many years after I was born. 1981. The Minnesota Twins played 109 games during the regular season. But they lost more games, finishing in seventh place overall. It was my favorite shirt that Dad owned because he wore it all the time. He loved baseball. Before I was born, he played on North Division's Blue Devils baseball team in high school. He would have loved to see me play first pitch, but I was Miss Gelatin Hands, clumsy, and threw like a girl.

As much as I loved being inside Dad's arms, I remember him appearing and then disappearing at will. The jingling noise the keys made when he inserted them into the key fob awakened me in the night. I'd run to him. I'd smell stale French fries coming from his uniform as he held me, greeting me from the front door. In my memory, I also see visions of my parents arguing and fighting all the time about Dad not being home at night. But, examining my family and me, you would never really know. It was as if nothing else in the world mattered more to my parents than me.

I was the only child for about eighteen months before Tasha was born. And, for a while, I thought I would forever be Dad's number one girl. I guess I am, in a way. I mean, I am Dad's firstborn.

Now and then, when I think about that day when I first locked eyes with Dad, I look up at the eight-by-ten-inch photograph of the three of us captured in time. A time when all I had were Mama and Dad, and all they had was me. A photo where a father shows love to the woman in his arms. He is nurturing. He is joy. He is the air I breathe. He will help coach his baby girl through Army boot camp. And he would also coach his first daughter through every roller-coaster, even heartbreak.

PART ONE

VIRGINIA

She stood there resolutely. The shuffling from my brother dragging his feet as he tried to keep up with Mama pulling his little hand, the leaves scattering from Tasha's moccasins, the long walk up ahead to the Route 62 bus stop that kept getting longer, the sucking of Mama's teeth as she reacted to my questions—that all left my nine-year-old curiosity in limbo. "What happened to your Mama and Daddy? Why did they take you away from them? Do you remember how they looked? What did they look like?" She grew cold feet trying to pass over a difficult moment. It was the first time I'd seen Mama not herself as if she was somewhere else.

The awkward silence grew tall like a wall between the both of us. I could only hear every engine in the Brew City raging as we ate dust, and the instant slamming of screeching brakes. The traffic lights flashed red then green. We moved briskly in Mama's silence.

It was a mystery when it was Mama's turn to talk about herself. She was never completely attentive to my yearning for love. With each idle minute that passed, I grew more suspicious as I studied the diminishing sparkle that had once lit her eyes. I thought of her family often. I assumed they were long gone. They were no longer here. They were never there when it counted. That's why the clouds hovered over Mama's shoulders as she walked. I could feel the coldness of Mama's footsteps through my bones. It was uncomfortable the way the weather was angry; even the Wisconsin trees were bitter, and lonely like her.

I felt goosebumps. The wind whisked away the crusted leaves that tumbled across the ground making me imagine what the life of a motherless child must be like—chasing scattered leaves.

As we continued our journey towards Route 62 on Capital Drive, the heavy air sprinkled the tips of our noses with scents of citrus and sulfur. I pulled my hat down to fully cover my frozen ears. I kept close watch just in case Mama had a change of heart.

She didn't. Something focused her dreamy eyes away from mine and held them there. Maybe it was the oak tree just up ahead, extremely tall, copper with a wide canopy. Or maybe it was the struggle to keep a grip on my little brother's hand as he weaseled away like a wet wiggly worm while she pretended everything was wonderful.

We scurried on. We didn't want to miss Route 62, the route my Grandpa Zeke Sr. took for work. It would be another twenty to thirty minutes before we'd see another bus, and there would be no guarantee that Grandpa Zeke Sr. would be driving it. We rode the bus every day, but that day, we never returned home.

Before we crossed the street on Capitol Drive, I held onto Tasha's hand. We were conjoined twins at the hip, only I wore pink, and she wore blue. The busy cars either moved forward in passing or made a sharp turn in front of us. Tasha and I looked both ways. And then back to Mama. She nodded. The coast became clear. We felt the adrenaline rush as we attempted to do something children shouldn't be doing alone—crossing a busy intersection. We leaped across the wide road with clammy hands and crooked smiles to the opposite side of the street as if we'd suddenly won a race. Before we lunged onto the sidewalk, we splashed our boots into a small puddle and celebrated with a victory dance because we'd made it, all by ourselves, across such a busy street. Then, on the other side of the road, we waited for Mama as she continued to struggle with our brother's stubborn hand. While Mama and Jay-Jay lagged a few steps behind, Jay-Jay loved to kick the acorns on the ground, then watch them tumble and scatter. Tasha and I sang silly songs, hopping in circles, and stumbling on sloppy feet until the bus came scurrying down the slopes of an uneven road.

The Route 62 bus pulled up in front of us, its doors flung ajar. "Grandpaaa!" We dragged the last "a" in his name as a sweet, sappy song. We plunged up three steps. Grandpa Zeke Sr. rested his hand over the slot where you insert the money into the machine. I hugged Grandpa in passing and caught a whiff of his Brut aftershave cream and Spearmint breath reminding me of the times when Dad would wrap me inside his coat during the cold months. I felt his heart beating next to mine. I sat within Grandpa's peripheral vision while he drove the bus. Darting for the first row of worn seats, I propped myself up onto the cracked pleather, beating Tasha to the large window. Mama would only allow us to sit near the front of the bus. I didn't know what it was about the back of the bus that drew us there like flies to the forbidden fruit. But she made it clear that we didn't belong there.

It felt so cozy on the bus. My fragile hands became instantly warm. I swatted off my mittens and stuffed them deep inside my pockets. Mama talked to Grandpa for what seemed like hours, mainly about Grandpa's day and how we often misbehaved as her children... blah, blah, blah. I blew my breath onto the window until I saw clumps of gray matter resting on the glass. With my pointer finger, I drew dainty stick figures—one of me, one of Tasha, and one of Jay-Jay holding hands. I drew us smiling. No matter what we had gone through, we were always smiling, always clean, and well-behaved, except for Jay-Jay.

And if I closed my eyes and focused hard enough, I could imagine our stick figures standing outside of one of those brick homes or the ones with white vinyl paneling with wreaths hanging on the doors as the bus went by—the pleasant homes near the upper side of Capitol Drive, where the higher the street numbers got, the nicer the neighborhoods were, the larger the doors, the cleaner the lawns with no bald patches amid overgrown grass, only apple green lawns and peach fuzz trees. Some houses even had white picket fences with tall posts standing at attention.

My perfect house, I imagined, was white with large bay windows and black shutters. I loved the red doors and fancy gold numbers that were donned upon them. An Oxford mailbox post stood near the street corner, matching the shutters and the structured picket fence. The details of the white wooded fence surrounded the house like a row of foot soldiers. The poise stature was distinguished evenly as spaced vertical boards and the pickets attached to horizontal rails. I imagined the family who lived behind such a fence never had to worry about carrying the heavy burdens of their mothers, the shame of moving from place to place, and leaving behind prized possessions, and other things they couldn't carry along. The fence kept out the people disguised as angels with lion's teeth and beastly eyes.

There's a treehouse in my backyard surrounded by Gloriosa daisies, marigolds, yarrow, and pineapple lilies. Dream-walking through the mysteriously deep lemon-lime grass with sprinkles of sunshine, I realized I was made for this life—no troubles, no stress, just me, a tire swing hanging from a large oak tree and nature, plenty of nature all around my white picket fence.

Instead, there were no pictures of our family hanging on Mama's walls. No still images of crooked smiles and missing front teeth. No legacy was left behind from the Washington side of the family. I found that strange. No camera. No trace. We were a family that didn't keep pictures around the house but least at Grandma Lizz and Grandpa Zeke Sr.'s house— Dad's parents—there were always pictures headlining the walls, especially photographs taken on holidays. Grandma Lizz and Grandpa Zeke Sr. have kept many albums of photos over the years. And every moment I had the opportunity to, I studied them all.

I always wondered why Mama never talked about her family. She must have forgotten them, sometime long ago, I was afraid. All the anxious thoughts of the lost family made my brain dribble, so I tried to not think about Mama growing up in foster care. I knew it was Mama growing up in foster care that created a wedge between her children. As the bus quickly brushed by the many houses that I imagined we lived in, I realized that Mama was the only person I knew who grew up that way. I wondered if she was loved any less. I wondered why I never felt her affection, the warmth of a hug, the softness of a gentle peck on the cheeks. I wondered why she wouldn't want her own children to experience what she couldn't. My brain has hit the maximum rebounds on any resolution of playing the blame game.

I felt a lot of loveless nights at bedtime when my eyes met darkness. My faded Rainbow Bright comforter was my refuge in times of trouble. My pillowcase stuffed with our old clothes welcomed me. The hallway light soothed me. Knowing my sister shared the same bed and she never wet it eased me. I also felt like there was a missing link to end the day, something more than 9:00 PM illuminating from the top of the dresser and eerie shadows swaying outside of the bedroom window. Something more than hearing the front door close, the key turning to lock, and the footsteps heading down the stairs, and straight to the club or tavern a few blocks away. Something more than scaly walls in a cheap duplex rental where the paint was plastered thick as concrete, like hot grease splattered on the wall, lost in a realm of opaque beige in the nudity of the wall, revealing scars. Something more than being mindlessly stuck inside of muddy sand.

For the rest of the bus ride, I pressed my forehead against the window, covering our stick figures as I gently closed my eyes, and dreamed about my perfect family in my perfect house, of being submerged in all the hidden natural beauty in my backyard. Then Mama's voice called out. "It's our stop." I jumped up with a yawn, kissed my Grandpa Zeke Sr. goodbye, as I scampered off the bus, and fully awakened to the uncertainty the real world brings.

Sightseeing became the norm for my siblings and me growing up. Mama took us out window shopping when we rode the city bus. And we often rode Grandpa Zeke Sr.'s bus route all afternoon long, listening to his interpretation of the good old days when things cost pennies on the dollar. Sometimes Mama would give us twenty-five cents, and sometimes, we would get fifty cents. For twenty-five cents, I could get a variety of items from the corner store. I could get a bag of chips, and twenty-five pieces of penny candies, or I could get one peppermint stick, one Jolly Rancher, and five pieces of penny candies. For fifty cents, I usually picked out a bag of chips and a small fruit juice barrel, or I picked out donuts and a fruity drink. In the 1930s, Grandpa Zeke Sr. probably had a variation of everything for just about a nickel, right before he'd go into how he'd chop wood. Seemed like they worked harder than we ever had to do as kids—we were city kids. The closest I had ever been to a farm was on a field trip where I learned how to milk a cow.

All things mattered, the simple views of life. He saw it beautifully as he drove all over the city, and so did I as his passenger. Even the abandoned buildings with broken windows, and stained walls surrounded by trashed lots were reminiscent of times when factory jobs boomed like the sight of the Hully Gully performed outside a jammed juke joint at 2:00 AM. It's strange how familiar places changed but their memories felt the same.

I will never forget the day we left home. After many years, I still hold onto the memories of being a castaway. I remember the day all too well. We didn't even have breakfast.

"Get up quickly. Get your things ready. It's time for us to go. Now!"

"Why, Mama? Why do we have to go?"

"Because we have to."

"But why? I don't wanna go. We are always leaving."

"Because I said so, that's why. Go get ready. Now!"

I pouted. I stomped my feet on each stair until I grabbed my things—We were always running from something. I hated leaving so abruptly. By the time I came down, I saw Mama leaning against the window at the front of the house with Tasha and Jay-Jay right beside her. I walked past the all-white living room where plastic covered the white furniture outlined in wood trimming. I heard Mama say something about someone from the shelter being here. With our heads hung low, we each headed to the mudroom and out the front door in a single-file formation. I felt the pins and needles from being forced from our home. Grandma Lizz followed closely behind to see our way out. A white mystery van parked out front to take us to an unfamiliar place to rest our heads at night.

I imagined her to be the devil with piercing brown eyes who showed up in a mystery van and approached the front door. She walked with a sense of purpose. She was petite but frightening. She was coming to collect our souls. This devil I imagined wore her hair brushed back into a clean, weepy ponytail. I didn't notice her horns. They shined like 14-karat gold over silver. Instead of greeting this ominous being, I covered my eyes. I wished the doors opened to the sight of Grandpa Zeke Sr. smiling with his hand hovering over the money slot of the bus's pay machine. If only we were going for a familiar city bus ride like we always did when we window-shopped. Then, I gasped for clean air, but the enemy suffocated me holding its tricks. The outdoors felt so heavy. My size four feet couldn't move. I felt intoxicated with sorrow and submerged by the weight of the world my family would soon face out there alone. My tears warped me into her dimension—only there were mirrors all around me, and all I saw was myself staring back at the rendition of me.

When we met the dark cloud hovering over the clipboard containing the book of names, evil revealed what souls she was sent to collect. I saw Grandma Lizz sit down on her nice outdoor chair in the mudroom just outside of her off-limits white room. She was safe from the darkness. It was Mama the presence wanted. Grandma Lizz's face was stone cold. I glared back at her pleading, why? "I want to stay here with you." "Go with your mom," she ordered. Then, I recognized her eyes, the same idle eyes that Mama once had. They never met mine, either. Is it possible that Grandma summoned this she-devil? I wondered what fate lay ahead for us. Would we be split up too, like Mama and her siblings in their youth? That aint nuthin but the devil. I thought.

I followed her and her book of names along with Mama, Tasha, and Jay-Jay. We went one after the other, marching down Grandma Lizz's narrow walkway out in front of the old house to soon find out our fate. No wonder Mama never spoke about foster care. Nobody wanted us. Nobody cared. Grandpa Zeke Sr. was working. Dad was always working. Why wasn't my plea for mercy working?

After all, Mama was not my paternal grandma's daughter. And that day, the nature of our relationship showed—we'd been booted out, tossed on the streets like empty bottles. The screen door slammed behind us sealing the deal. Grandma Lizz watched from the many windows surrounding the mudroom. As we pulled off the passenger van, I realized we were on our own to figure things out. I tried to soak up my puddle of tears with the soles of my feet, but my heart wouldn't let me.

And, suddenly, the same houses I would see when riding on Grandpa Zeke Sr.'s bus route quickly faded away. Each shape of the houses shifted into some other form. The doors were smaller, lacking living luster. No welcome mats or beautiful wreaths at the door. The grass in the front yards of each house had bald patches of dirt amid overgrown weeds held captive. Chain-link fences surrounded each perimeter. I couldn't imagine myself there, no more than I could imagine myself lost. At the moment, I couldn't imagine myself anywhere but my Grandpa Zeke Sr.'s city bus, Route 62.

I knew I felt as though I was not wanted, but Mama must have been feeling much worse. I wondered if she felt as abandoned as I did. I wondered if she felt any humiliation. I wondered if my sister and brother caught on to what was happening. They went along; they never spoke a word.

I remembered little about the shelter, only the long dim halls. The bathroom door screeched as footsteps pounded the fretted floors further down the hall. There was a curfew, 9 o'clock PM. The many cots were spread throughout the unfamiliar room, with boys and girls segregated in sleeping quarters. I remembered the bland veggies and lumpy mashed potatoes served in the cafeteria. I barely ate. And I remembered being cold in the middle of the night. I had such a thin blanket —it felt scratchy against my skin. I remembered checking the door, making sure the boogeyman wasn't creeping through the hallway. I thought about the dark cloud and the list of names on the clipboard, and what home would be disrupted next. I thought a lot about my brother, who slept across the hall in the separate room designated for male children. He was five. No one tucked him in at night. Lastly, I thought about Grandma Lizz. I wondered if it was worth my shame.

I remembered we went to school the next day feeling like nothing. I was nobody. I was uninspired. I was embarrassed. I quietly sat in the squeaky chair at my desk in the back row of the class anticipating when Dad was coming to save the day. And when he didn't show up at the end of the day, I imagined Dad trying to find us. I imagined he felt just as hopeless. If only I left behind a note for Dad to find.

I had only one friend in Mrs. Hunter's fifth-grade class, a friend from Laos, Seng. Seng sat beside me. She stared at me. I looked down at the floor. The school bell rang violently. It startled me. Before Seng began to ask what the matter was, the class opened with the morning announcements. Thank God, I thought I was saved by the bell.

…Today, for lunch, we are having baked chicken and mashed potatoes and peas and assorted fruit cups, and an oven-baked roll…

Aaaah! Okay. It sounded better than shelter food; I wondered if it was truly better. Each food item at Women's Hope Center had the same unsatisfying taste: cold and bland.

Next, I stood up from my chair, placing my hand over my heart, pledging my allegiance to a dusty flag hanging in the corner at the front of the classroom, focusing sternly on the cobwebs hanging from the speaker box instead of reciting all the words to the pledge. I brooded. Seng could never know. I didn't want to talk about what we were facing. She wouldn't understand. She wouldn't want a homeless person as a friend.

I tried my best to not look homeless when picking out my outfit to wear to school. We didn't have any clothes. The shelter provided donated clothes. The residents rummaged through the bags of gently used donated clothing like vultures. My siblings and I picked from what was left over while Mama watched. I timidly grabbed a thin white buttoned-down blouse, a thick white cable sweater, white belt, and a pair of frosted denim jeans. For the first time, I felt like a ghost.

The sound coming from the xylophone played for four keys. I plopped down in my seat and picked up my pencil to doodle on scrap paper. I ignored Seng's questions about why Mama and I appeared so sad that day. "You know you can talk to me," Seng suggested. I kept my head hung low, my eyes cemented to my squiggly lines and stick creatures. *She's just being nice.* I must have convinced myself for my own comfort. Although, in my mind, I tried to imagine riding the city bus to see all the houses I dreamed about living in. But I could only see blurred lines with Jay-Jay somewhere tangled in the middle and the smell of musty pong on worn bus seats.

Although my childhood memories of Mama were synonymous with surviving, I learned about the significance of a women's shelter shortly after our stay. They had programs to help a single mother get back on her feet, even if it was only for a little while. I think I realized then that a single mother had to be strong even though she appeared feeble.

I don't remember how long we were displaced. It seemed like an eternity fell by my waist side. I also don't recall ever seeing the devil gripping the book of names again. I only prayed that God would keep my siblings and me off the hit list. My understanding of our situation grew when we exited the white passenger van for the definitive time. Social services have a job to do even though the process can be a living nightmare while they do it. We had a life we thought we knew ripped from us and replaced with another in a matter of minutes. The van pulled up to an upper-level duplex on Center Street near an alleyway and Lavarnway Boys & Girls Club. We had our own four walls, a roof, and a locked door. It was our place to call home. No more sleeping beside strangers. No more running trying to beat the 9:00 PM curfews and losing out on a bed.

I thought we would never see Dad or his family again. Mama was often private with our adventures. Our business was just that, her business. I often fantasized about Dad taking us away, and we'd live happily ever after like in a fairy tale. I couldn't help but be disappointed when it didn't happen, but I was never angry. I grew sad, but never bitter. I understood Dad must have had his reasons. Although he was not perfect, he was perfect enough for me. I don't know if it was because of my whining and complaining about not seeing Dad, but one day Dad's Cadillac was parked outside our duplex. It wasn't banana like how I remembered; it was white with power windows. He stopped by on the weekends, at least every other one. He brought my siblings and me allowance dressed in a white envelope with our names written on the front every other Friday. The amount correlated to our ages. I thought nine dollars was all the money in the world.

Mama often revisited the saying blood is thicker than water. After all, we needed a family; we didn't have much family on her side. "Children should always know who their people are, regardless of how the adults feel about each other," Mama said. She believed that even after all that she had been through—different foster homes as a child, the long month spent in the women's shelter, the denial of my sister from Grandma Lizz denying my sister as her granddaughter (Tasha was too fair-skinned). Still to her, the family would always be the most important thing despite the hurt, and even when she could seldom stand the ground Grandma Lizz walked on. However, Mama's ideology of family ties made keeping a close connection to Dad's side of the family a lot easier in theory—we had no one else. But, in the back of my mind, I always wondered why it was so easy for Grandma Lizz to let us go, her own grandchildren, her own flesh and blood. She let us go away with a perfect stranger holding a clipboard with piercing eyes and a tiny waist. She let her drive us away. Maybe it was tough love, maybe not. Maybe it was us—we didn't fit in; we were never good enough.

I thought the reason Mama struggled so much in life was that she did not have her biological parents to show her the epitome of real love. Mama's biological parents had over a dozen children. Mama at least shared that much before she would completely shut down when I prompted her to tell me more.

On a typical Saturday, we made our way downtown to the Grand Avenue Mall. Excitement took over me because I knew we didn't have to window shop this trip. It was allowance weekend from Dad. My sister and I were wearing similar light jackets. I wore pearly pink; she wore bright blue. Mama pulled Jay Jay's soiled solid sleeve from having it stuffed in his mouth. As we walked up the curved road to the bus stop Tasha turned to me and sang, "Step on a crack, you'll break your Mama's back."

I nodded and we kept skipping over the lines cemented every three steps into the sidewalk. When I grew tired, I asked Mama, "So why did you and your sisters and brothers go to foster homes?" Mama must have felt that ten years old was old enough to know better.

She responded, "Irma had a lot of kids she couldn't take care of us, and our father was a drunk. They just couldn't take care of us." Mama continued to march straight ahead like it didn't bother her to finally say it. Tasha and I continued jumping over those lines in the path because our family didn't need any more bad luck, especially if something were to happen to Mama. We were superstitious like that. Thanks to Mama's fine parenting. A black cat once crossed a few feet ahead of us and Mama yelled, "Yall spit on the ground and hurry up. Don't look back at me, just do it." And so, we did in unison. Then Mama said, "You'll get bad luck if you don't."

I never liked cats much after that. I never knew why Irma was unfit. Even with my young mind, I knew that unfit was bad enough to be tossed away. It was probably ludicrous to have all those kids, even after they were plucked one by one from beneath her wings. I wondered if Irma ever knew to spit when she saw a black cat?

Irma was short for Armmie. The names Irma and Herman seemed pleasant, loving, and normal, like a nice couple from a 1960s sitcom. I imagined a stay-at-home parent and a hard-working man, maybe a construction worker or an entrepreneur, perhaps someone who you can tell was industrious by the grease, grit, and grime on his hands. I imagined a couple that would never have their children taken away. I totally imagined my life to have a different plot. I wished I knew better.

"Mama, why don't you have pictures of when you were born?"

"When we were sent to foster care, we were sent with a picture. I don't know what happened to it. It was in our things; when we ran away, we must've left it," Mama said.

I asked Mama, "What did my Grandma Irma look like in the picture?"

"I remember she had very dark skin, a wide nose, and she was a big woman with thick hair. Our foster mother showed us a newspaper article about a lady and a man and all their kids in the picture. Our foster mother asked me, do you think the woman in the picture is beautiful? Do you want to be like the woman in the picture? And I answered, yes to both questions. I don't know why I said yes. I just did. And I'm so glad I did. Because that woman in the photo was our mother, Irma."

"I wish we could get that article one day."

"We were the first triplets born at that hospital in Milwaukee," Mama said. She must have been in a good mood to give me such insight with a bright smile. I saw heaven in her eyes.

The bus screeched to a halt. The doors flung open. The heat from the bus smacked me in the face. I noticed the driver wasn't Grandpa. Instead, it was an older lady. I wasn't allowed to talk to strangers, so I pulled out my change from my jean skirt pocket and sprinkled the coins into the money machine. I enjoyed watching the machine count down the money inserted and the jingles the coins made. I waited for the bus lady to rip me off a transfer slip for another bus ride later in the day.

When we found our seats close to the front of the bus, Mama promised us a trip to the library sometime soon. She said the library can help us find the picture of her family. We never made it, though. I don't know why I always believed her. She was good at making promises she could never keep. So, I promised myself that I would one day follow through. I would find the article Mama referenced if it killed me.

I guess I was hoping to find a black-and-white time capsule of Irma and Herman surrounded by all their offspring. I guess I was hoping to find Irma cradling the two baby girls in each arm, and Herman sitting on the seat next to the hospital bed, smiling over the baby boy in his arms. The other kids hovered over the rails on each side of the bed. They all had Herman's wide nose and Irma's thick Nigerian hair. I guessed. I hoped. Then, I wandered off.

I wandered back to a place where there was a white picket fence—outside the big red door where the family welcomed the newly-born triplets. I envisioned the father checking mail inside the Oxford mailbox that matched the color of the shutters. The mother would be inside the white house, sitting in front of the large bay windows reading the Sunday paper on crisp floral furniture, next to the triplets nesting inside of their individual bassinets. The older kids would be playing out back in a nice yard with a treehouse that stood up in the middle of the yard, before CPS, before they both were negligent parents.

Before I was even thought of. Before I was only a speck in my father's eye, I came from a perfect family of strangers.

LIZZIE MAY

On a neatly folded, special piece of paper, a time capsule of my family's origins displays pastel pinks, Hybrid Tea roses, and fancy calligraphy. Featured was Lizzie May Parker, born in Blytheville, Arkansas, to the union of Earskin and Martha Riley. As a young adult, Lizzie May worked in the cotton fields when she met my grandpa, Zeke Parker Sr., who was the love of her life. The two were married when they later migrated from Missouri to Milwaukee to live out the rest of their lives in a home they would never compromise or sell.

I always wondered why the bulk of my family settled near the heart of the dairy city. My grandpa and grandma were originally country folks, but they traded the country for city living in Milwaukee. Of all the cities they could have moved to, they migrated to a place known for cows, cheese, Miller beer, and serial killers—and let's not forget Harley Davidson motorcycles. Their way of life began to change when we, their grandchildren, were born. Grandma and Grandpa became more socially conservative. After spending ten years in the military service, I would say most Mid-westerners I knew were more like that—family-oriented, religious, passive-aggressive, even.

One day, when I couldn't have been more than seven or eight years old—I complained about a task I had to complete when my grandma happened to be sitting there reading her *Journal Sentinel.* Grandma folded down on the corner of her newspaper.

"You kids don't know anything about hard work. You all just don't know how good you've got it. Now, your grandma and grandpa had it hard. Right, Zeke?"

"Yeah, that's right, Lizz," Grandpa said.

Here it comes, I thought, *the civil rights speech.*

"My mother carried me on her back while she picked cotton. You know I picked cotton as a little girl? THAT was hard work! We picked cotton 'till our hands bled," she said. And Grandpa continued to nod his head in agreement with his wise wife.

I should have known better than to complain about washing dishes or sweeping the floor for even a second. I would automatically receive a twenty-minute lecture on how their generation had it harder than Millennials, or should I say Gen Xers—I am somewhere in between. I do admit that my generation tends to seriously complain about minimal tasks. However, when I have thousand-plus things to do in one day, venting about the insignificant tasks for a few seconds can help release the tension before executing what seems like endless work—at least it does for me, anyway. But that was Grandma Lizz, a natural-born leader who had no time for excuses.

It's funny how you never really know the fine details about a person until you're sitting up one night studying their obituary. Like, I never knew how old my grandmother was. "A lady never tells her age. You don't ask; it's rude," Grandma always declared. She'd aged like sea glass, naturally weathered with a smooth, glistening edge.

I didn't make it up to Grandma's funeral in Milwaukee. I thought I would feel something like sadness or utter shame for not attending or even remorse about my absence. But I didn't. And I don't. It's been a full year since we said our goodbyes. But, now and then, I think about small moments with her. After all, she is the woman who introduced me to Folger's coffee at any hour of the day. She is the woman who draped her pearls around my neck when I attended prom. She is the only woman for whom I would don the name "Grandma." She's the only grandma I have ever known.

I have three sisters and two brothers from Dad, and we've grown over the years to become the black sheep of the family. My half-sister Brittany sent me a copy of Grandma Lizz's obituary. She sent it in a text. Nobody bothered to send one in the mail. To be fair, I wasn't looking for one, either. Staring at it now, I can't help but notice that it's awfully frilly. Pepto-Bismol pink—not a color she kept around the house or even had in her wardrobe growing up. It was a shade that belonged in the medicine cabinet instead of printed on fancy cardstock. The colors more suitable for Grandma Lizz would have been black and white with bold, golden letters like the Grand Madame she was. Right or wrong, there were never any gray areas in how she lived her life. She ushered at her Baptist church; people treated her like precious gold. She lived a full life, outliving two of her sons—Dad and Uncle Tyrone, who both died of cancer. And that alone was extremely hard for her.

On the front cover of her obituary, Grandma's smile is so bright which tells me that her last moments were of joy. In other photos, she was a cold stone. But in her obituary, she's different. I've never seen this side of her captured before. Here, the curl of her lips is full of concealed threats, making her look like a fawn holding a machete. If I didn't know any better, I would have thought she was the mastermind of a home invasion and had just gotten away with it. The Lizzie May I knew would have just finished fussing with her doctors about discharge day because their medical expertise was not to her standard, therefore inadequate. In her final days, she wore one of those hospital gowns that were thin as paper. It tied around the neck and exposed her from behind. Beneath her gown, cords protruded through the outdated fabric. She wore that gown as if she were the belle of the ball, the way that one shoulder appeared slightly elevated than the other. Grandma was a showstopper, a superstar amongst the medicine pink flowers and elegant font that highlighted various versions of her.

I wish I could talk to the lady portrayed smiling in each photo without becoming angry or bitter about the past. The nostalgia after her passing began to regress to uncomfortable feelings of disappointment from all her rejections, judgments, and harsh criticisms—including all the family gatherings when she poked her nose in where it didn't belong, and the time when she sent my siblings and me off to live in a homeless shelter with our mama. I thought I'd made my peace with Grandma Lizz the day Dad died several months before COVID-19 wreaked havoc over the world. It was there at Froedtert Hospital, when he died, that I realized Grandma, the Grand Madame always had to be in control of everything and everyone. She wore the pants and swung the ax, while the rest of us hang on for the ride in cheap skirts and worn heels.

The last time I spoke with Grandma was on her death-bed. I asked one of my sisters to call me once she'd made it over to Grandma's house. Brittany called me on the phone when she arrived a few hours later so that I could have one more moment with her.

"Hi Grandma," I said, once Brittany passed the phone to her.

"Hi baby," she said in her raspy voice.

"I graduated again."

"Yay!" Grandma cheered.

I smiled at the thought of her dentures hitting her high cheekbones. I didn't know what else to say. I just wanted her last moments with me to be proud. I probably should have asked her about her day or something. But that was pointless, considering Grandma was confined to a bed with medicine and oxygen machines. My mind drew a blank, trying to conjure up meaningful last words. Then, I suddenly remembered what Grandma would say when she had nothing nice to say. She'd say, "Love anyway." I thought about myself, how hard it was for me to do that, to just love anyway, despite the hurt bottled up with nowhere to go. I knew I needed to release the past, to forgive, but not forget.

No. Scratch that. Instead, I wanted to ask her, why did you let my siblings and me go to a homeless shelter with our unstable mama? How could you let us—your own flesh and blood—walk out the door like that? Why didn't you tell Mama to go alone and let us stay home, with you and

Grandpa? Why couldn't you have just called Dad instead and demanded he take us? Still, I said it:

"I love you, Grandma."

"I love you too, baby," she said.

There was a brief silence until the background chatter called for distraction. All the buzz sounded like worker bees as everyone flocked for a final taste of sweet honey. You could say it was a swarm of goodbyes. I don't know who had the best farewell to the Queen Bee, but I only know it wasn't me.

I never prepared a farewell speech of what I would say to her near the end. I'm sure other family members held better memories of Grandma Lizz. She always thought she should die at home among family in her own home, on her own terms. And I didn't blame her. I would want to die somewhere familiar among loved ones, too. Hospitals are scary, especially now amid a global pandemic. Although I didn't attend the funeral, I still miss my grandma, no matter what we'd been through.

Only I became emotionally exhausted and detached from Grandma during our last real visit. I was tired of Grandma's bitching, gripes, and complaints—tired of her telling the doctors about Dad's prognosis, diagnosis, and treatment plans. I was tired of what came after death: traveling hundreds of miles when folks would never use those same miles to see about me; the overzealous funeral arrangements; the depleting bank account from dining out and hotel fees; grieving everyone we'd lost already, then hugging family—hugging seemed like embracing complete strangers, forcing a smile, pretending—tired of so much pretending to care when really, what I wanted to say was screw them all. Instead, I let my mind wander off someplace else, with the bluest water, warm sand, large umbrellas, and ice cream sundaes.

When I think of Grandma, I often try to think about the brown bungalow nesting mid-block on Capitol Drive. And then I think about my grandpa and how much love the two of them had for one another. My grandparents were married for well over fifty years—real love—and had six children together: Diana, Zeke Jr., Tyrone, Karen, Michelle, and I can't forget about Clint. Uncle Clint and I are just a few months apart. Imagine the agony in my voice trying to explain how I am months older than my uncle. Mothers and grandmothers shouldn't be pregnant at the same time.

Grandpa Zeke Sr. drove Route 62 for many years up and down Capitol Drive before he retired. Next to Dad, Grandpa was my favorite parent. His health hasn't been the best over the years—Grandpa has one of those mechanical hearts. It didn't help that Grandpa Zeke Sr. smoked for years before completely giving up his Newport. Sadly, when he rests in eternal peace, my aunts will probably sell the old house and split the profit between them. Typical adult children. They don't recognize the true value of anything. They don't see the house the way that I do—stoic, made of strong bones, and with a rich family history.

Before the move to Milwaukee, my grandparents had worked on a farm. Shortly after arriving in Milwaukee, they purchased the old house on Capitol Drive. It was the house that Dad grew up in, the house I grew up in, and the house I brought my children home annually to visit. The old house, that cradled the middle of the neighborhood, they had purchased for pennies on a dollar. The old house was the first piece of real property my family owned.

My fonder memories were of that house—Grandma's legacy. The old house appeared to be cradled in the middle of the block like a kid tucked between both parents, looking out into the world. The surrounding windows jutted out like body armor, and the roof hovered over all four walls like my guardian angel. The mudroom out front was where only adults could sit as they watched small children run back and forth across the cracked sidewalks. A long driveway trailed to the back entrance.

Grandma Lizz and Grandpa Zeke Sr. never had a working doorbell. When we visited, three thuds on the side window prompted Grandma's furry dog, Scottie, to bark ferociously—although he was small and couldn't harm a fly. Grandpa would greet the family at the door with happy eyes as if he hadn't seen us in years. Something was always cooking on the stove. The aroma of fried chicken, collard greens, cornbread dressing, homemade lemon pies, and pound cakes filled our tiny noses. The house wasn't much; it was not larger than a racquetball court. Still, it was treated like an heirloom, a place where everyone gathered to visit from near and far during the holidays, where it welcomed three generations of family.

I thought I was the lucky one, living at Grandma's house my senior year in high school. I was ecstatic because I finally had my space and no younger siblings to look after. Dad had approved of the move because I was the oldest, therefore, the most independent. My grandparents kept the plastic stars that illuminated the dark on the ceiling of the attic, the stars I attached to the wall above my twin bed out in the open space where my dreams manifested. The stars I glared at when I pounced back onto my bed, often in deep thought of my future with my arms supporting the back of my head, twenty-five years ago. And each star reminded me of all the places I would go and experience because of what I learned while at Grandma's house.

Lances of sun-scorched grassy backyard fueled the summer months at the old house. All weekend long, we would play as we ran around, wetting one another with a Super Soaker, or my favorite game, *Little Sally Walker*. We'd make a circular motion and challenge one another with a dance in the circle. And the best became *Little Sally Walker*. We'd play several rounds of *Ring Around the Rosie*, joining hands in a complete circle. I'd feel dizzy, and then finally, we'd all fall, our knees brushing the grass.

When the clouds mirrored the waist-deep snow in winter months we'd make perfect snow forts and large snowmen. Grandchildren sailed across cardboard boxes or lids from the green trash cans down the snowy banks one after another, prompting real fun—we didn't have the internet or other forms of technology.

My family celebrated Thanksgiving, Christmas, Easter Sunday, and the Fourth of July at the old house. All the grandchildren crammed like sardines into the sitting area right in front of a floor-modeled boxed television screen. Remote control-less, a pair of pliers cranked up some of our most-watched karate and Western shows. And a U-shaped piece of a wire hanger extended from the opening of an old damaged VCR to play *Willow* and *The Dark Crystal*. We all enjoyed it until the VHS tapes no longer played the same.

"Grandpaaa, the movie is not working," my cousins and I would pout.

"What you mean it's not working? Then, what's it doing?"

"It's glitching, Grandpa."

"Let me take a look at it."

Grandpa would come in from the kitchen into the living room. He'd open the slot on the VCR, press eject, and with his hot breath, blow inside the VCR player. Dust bunnies sprinkled out like confetti. Grandpa inserted the movie back into the player and pressed Play. Nothing but a blank screen. He'd push down on top of the VHS inside of the player, and the picture would instantly pop onto the screen.

"You did it!" We'd cheer. Only, moments later, the movie would inevitably quit again.

"I know exactly what we need."

Grandpa would shuffle around inside his kitchen junk drawer, returning with a piece of folded-up coat wire, wrapped in masking tape. He'd hold up the rigger in midair, showing us what I could do to help. He'd stick it smoothly into the VCR player, and it held the VHS down into place, clinging to the player. There'd be a clear picture of *Willow* playing on the screen, thanks to Mr. Fix-it. When I think of my grandpa, I think of his unconventional challenges for making things work properly around the house— after hearing Grandma nag from behind.

The old house on Capitol Drive seemed magical during the holidays. Every year we looked forward to the socks Grandma had for us under the Christmas tree. Twenty-two pairs of assorted sizes, colors, and designs, wrapped in fancy, shiny paper, for all the grandchildren. I loved the way that my grandparents exchanged gifts. I loved the way that Grandpa looked at Grandma after opening variations of the same plaid shirt he got from her every year.

I lied to Grandpa once in my entire life. It still eats me up when I think about it. I told him that I had handmade a small bus for him as a Christmas gift. I'd wrapped it and put it beneath the tree. When he opened the gift, he adored the bus because he believed I made it. But really, I purchased the figurine from the dollar store with my allowance. I often wondered if he knew that I didn't make it, that I wasn't talented enough to paint the vibrant colors and small details onto the ceramic bus. I often wondered what Grandpa would think about his granddaughter lying about such a small thing.

Now that I am forty, I want to tell Grandpa I didn't make the bus, especially since, every time we see one another, he always mentions the teeny tiny bus. Still, he always seems so proud. I just could never say the words "I'm sorry, I lied." I lied because I didn't want my grandpa to throw away the bus like Grandma did when she spring cleaned every few months. She would say there were way too many grandchildren to keep every trinket gifted to them at Christmas time. I figured that if I lied, they both wouldn't have the heart to throw away something handmade. I wanted the bus to be as special to him as the socks I received every Christmas Day.

Once a year, when I took military leave, Grandpa would always bring up the fact that he still had that bus. *It's really not that big of a deal*, I'd think to myself. *I lied. You can throw the thing away now. It's not so special, at least not anymore.* As if I couldn't have felt any worse, he'd go on to reference the stars I'd placed upon the ceiling up in the attic, right above my twin bed. How sweet—my grandparents kept those up, too. I felt like I didn't deserve to be praised. I was such a liar. The bus and the stars made Grandpa think of me, and he'd smile. He always wanted me to know that they were still there in the old house—right where I'd left them, even after all this time. So, of course, I couldn't tell Grandpa about the bus now. I'd get all misty-eyed.

I equate both the memories of the small bus and the glowing stars to moments spent at the old house and the promise I made to myself while stargazing at the ceiling. I told myself that I would one day leave home and venture out to see the world. When I joined the Army, Grandpa told me he was so proud of me. And I was also so proud of him. He'd migrated with Grandma and their small children from the Antebellum South with little education and retired as a city bus driver. When I think of city buses, I think of Grandpa; we'd spent so many hours together on the Milwaukee Public Transit System.

I was unfortunate to have only one living grandmother my entire life, Mrs. Lizzie May. I wish I knew what having two was like. I always wanted two sets of grandparents. It would have balanced me in a way. However, sometimes I felt that, if my other grandma, Irma, were still alive, I would have been even closer to her because she was the face of my mother, a version of me.

I often dreamed about her and how she may have looked. I imagined her terra cotta skin; her hefty waistline; a set of linebacker shoulders; wild and gone with the wind bushy hair; and big brown eyes bridging a wide gap over her broad nose. All I have of my maternal grandmother is a name on Mama's birth certificate. I wish I had a picture of Irma. If only she were alive when I was born. But, in the end, it didn't matter. I was my father's daughter.

My favorite room in the old house was the living room my grandmother had heavily decorated. In Lizzie May's living room, I often studied the black-and-white photo taken of her, Grandpa, Aunt Diana, Dad, Uncle Tyrone, and Aunt Karen. They'd planted the old photo up high on the center shelf, so it overlooked the room. I often wondered why my grandparents never cracked a smile. I'd study the significance in their eyes, and the way they embraced the smiling, smaller children carefully placed on their laps. Perhaps they were the faces of hardworking parents who provided for their children, and the smiles in their children's eyes were the ones that mattered.

Lizzie May's living room had all white furniture, covered in plastic, nesting on top of a white rug. Children never stepped foot in that room filled with collectibles and porcelain antiques. Our young eyes exalted the white room. I always wanted to play with Grandma's lamp on her side marble table. The lamp was also a huge doll dressed in Victorian attire with a large, lacey lampshade as her hat. I'd seen nothing like it before. Lizzie May always received compliments on how nice the room was. That space was her trophy. In some ways, it measured their earlier success on the farm.

Grandpa drove a long, forest green-colored car when he wasn't driving the city bus. We called it Grandpa's Batmobile. He always parked it in the driveway on the side of the house. The back of the car looked like it had wings reaching out from each side, and its body seemed to stretch across The Great Lakes, the back row seats as wide as all of Milwaukee County. Only the oldest of the grandchildren would pile in the back of the ride, seat beltless, cruising down I-94 to the state line—six pairs of knobby, scuffed knees in various shades of brown, swinging with joy.

My grandparents would regularly head to a convenience store on the state line to purchase scratch-offs and lottery tickets. There was nothing like crossing our fingertips, hoping Grandpa or Grandma would hit the jackpot. But we'd learn to settle for chocolate and vanilla swirl ice cream cones from Mickey D's. The day would have been fair, the snow melted away, making room for pastels once more after a winter's slumber.

My younger sister Tasha, baby brother Zeke Jr—we called him Jay-Jay for short—half a dozen cousins, and I would play outdoors until the streetlights turned on. We often had the time of our lives without a care in the world—only a ball, two cans, and a jump rope for a game of Double Dutch.

Jumping rope was a competitive rite of passage that inner-city girls embraced, like mastering the hula hoop for the very first time. If you couldn't jump rope, you turned the rope from over your head until your armpits burned, or you grew thirsty trying. The ropes towered over you like two golden arches as you leaped over the rope each time it swept you off your feet at the sound of a rhythmic beat. The epitome of *Black Girl Magic* was the elaborate tricks of swinging ropes, the rocking, steady rhythm, and the raking noise of the rope when it rolled against the rigid concrete.

I never learned the tricks and trades of jumping inside the rope, but I loved to watch the neighborhood pros. I was happy with my ability to jump until the count of twenty before I stumbled out. There was different freedom inside of the rope. It was more than how my hair defied gravity as I jumped; it was the tingling sensation I felt from the soles of my sandals up through my spine. I felt like I didn't need anyone's permission to be free. I could be unapologetically me.

The clouds were always in reach. The memories of jumping rope felt warm and safe. They reminded me of a sense of security from a community of extended family, neighbors, and friends who I trusted. Jumping rope reminded me of the cool, savory taste of freshly cut watermelon awaiting us on the picnic table out back, and the buzzing coming from Grandpa's lawn mower as he observed us playing while he cut the lawn.

The older girls down the street were the best inside of the ropes. Cars rode past the neighborhood with the windows down, their horns sounding off at all the colorful hair bows, and barrettes flying in the air like mini saucers. We soared in between the ropes cheering, our gum popping, and our feet pounding the hot pavement all day long.

The heat of mid-summer slowly baked us, while the sweat dripped from our denim like drizzling rain. It wouldn't be long before our clothes would become stuck like Velcro, and the smell of wet dogs reeked from our small bodies. Grandma would yell, "You all smell like outside," followed by, "Close my back door. You letting all my air out."

At the old house, Grandma also taught her granddaughters posture and poise. My cousins, sister, and I practiced strutting while balancing books on top of our heads like models across the living room floor. Some days, we drank a little coffee and wrote in journals. Grandma said we were to call the first entry "Rules to Live By, by Grandma Parker." I only remembered one rule though. It was more than likely prompted by what she read in her newspaper over coffee. It went a little something like this:

"If a man tries to talk to you, you run and dial 9-1-1!"

We laughed at ourselves across the floor. "But Grandma he ain't do nuthin." Grandma turned her nose in the air and with disdain, she repeated, "Run. And dial 9-1-1!"

Unsurprisingly, we didn't hear anything new. In our journals, we often jot down the rules about talking with boys—especially older guys preying on young girls. We'd sit up under Grandma's fresh pedicure, waiting for her to plunder the next rule. Grandma said, "If you kiss a boy, you will get pregnant." We giggled. Grandma made the lines on her forehead deepen. She further explained that kissing leads to other things. At the time, I never had a boyfriend. I still played with dolls. In class, when notes circled around the room, there was one note from a boy that made it over to me. I felt special. The note read: "Do you like me? Circle yes or no." I envisioned not Mama or Dad, but Grandma and the word "baby," so I wrote underneath my response: "Maybe."

In the kitchen with the black and white checkerboard floors, we recorded songs off the radio using a cassette tape, pressing down with two fingers simultaneously on both Record and Play buttons on the boom box Dad gifted me for Christmas. We wrote long lessons from Grandma on notebook paper with ragged edges, signing our names in cursive at the bottom of the page. The aroma from the roasted coffee tickled the tips of each nostril as the steam blew them sweet kisses.

It's kind of hard to believe that there would be any talks of selling Grandma Lizz's house. But here I am writing about my feelings of grief, sorrow, and so much disappointment.

My children's children will never grow up experiencing the awesome times at Grandma Lizz's house. They will never even remember the address or know how to locate it on a map. It will sell for less than it's worth, and another family will occupy its walls, or maybe it will become another empty lot on Milwaukee's Northside. Grandma Lizz's house became a testament to our lives. People are always preaching about preserving history. But history will be sold to the highest bidder and buried like corpse. And somehow everything I know, and all my childhood memories that traced back to Grandma Lizz's house, will all fade away. The brown bungalow is known as the old house. My beginning. My end. My grandma's house.

While many people rode trains when they migrated from the South during the Great Migration, I imagined my grandparents merging forward onto I-57 North, headed towards the Windy City, leaving behind the land where they'd once worked up a sweat as sharecroppers, a land where they'd once "picked cotton to their hands bled," so that I might one day write this piece that holds an incredibly special place in my heart.

GRANDPA ZEKE SR.

Grandpa sat in his old recliner chair like he usually did after he returned home from a long day of driving. Its painted pleather seat spiraled like a cracked egg. I was in awe of Grandpa. He'd work up quite the appetite. I liked watching him prepare for chow. A meticulous eater and a casual talker, he was often the last in the house to eat because of his work. Grandma prepared his plate before everyone dug in, and she kept his portion warm for when he arrived. I watched Grandpa set up his TV tray right from his chair. First, he hung the napkin loosely on top of his white undershirt that was neatly tucked into dark lounge pants. Next, he carefully placed silverware on each side of the plate, a knife on one side, fork, and spoon on the other. Then, he took a slow sip of his evening coffee before slicing the meatloaf into fourths on his plate. And before he tasted his meatloaf, he swept his cornbread through the mound of brown gravy and took a bite. Then, Grandpa said that when the city of Milwaukee opened driver jobs to Black people, the line to apply was miles long. He was one of the few men that was hired by the bus company. He belched and excused himself immediately afterward. I stood next to Grandpa's knee taking in every piece of his miracle, and the smell of Grandma's hot water cornbread. Grandpa loved Grandma's cornbread like he loved history, and so did I, never fully realizing that my grandparents were a part of it—a history I would seldom find in my books.

My happy moments came from seeing Grandpa cruise down Route 62. Riding the bus for the first time was a great experience for me. We took the bus from the Eastern side of Capital Drive to the transfer center which was somewhere in midtown Milwaukee. The route was one big loop around just a small fraction of the city, roughly three to four miles. One trip around was approximately one hour of the day. Grandpa gave us Spearmint-flavored gum from his uniform pocket. I popped gum until the sweetness expired as I people-watched those who came on board. The next best thing about riding the bus was the people-watching.

I remembered a man sitting three rows back on the left side of the bus. He was a slender man with dark shoulder-length hair, gentle eyes, and a soft beard. He reminded me of a white Jesus, but I knew that Jesus wouldn't carry cigarettes in his upper shirt pocket as that guy did. He kept looking around at people and talking to himself, almost like he was studying them, judging them even. Once we made eye contact, Mama noticed, and she popped me on the shoulder blade. The blow stung me but not enough to shed a tear. She said it was rude to stare at strangers. I turned away from the man only after he smiled at me. I saw his stained teeth, at least the ones he had left, and it bothered me because good boys and girls never get cavities. I asked Mama what she thought his food tasted like with teeth like his? She jerked my arm and then whispered, "I'm going to beat your ass when we get home." I started to worry. I hoped she would forget after a long day. I prayed she forgot that I couldn't keep still and not say a word like good kids do. To outsiders, it looked like Mama was the sweetest woman in the world. But little did they know Mama had a mean grip on a belt. We embarrassed each other. It was the first time I noticed that people were not what they seemed at first glance.

After I straightened up, I also noticed that the noisier people sat at the very back of the bus. They apparently knew each other, often talking over one another. All the weirdos normally sat in the middle. The front of the bus was usually reserved for old people lost in newspapers and magazines and was also designated for people stuck in wheelchairs. Sometimes the bus would be packed with all different types of passengers, with only standing room available, while other times we were Grandpa's only passengers. We'd sit close in the front seats. On an empty bus, we could explore the seats and the graffiti behind them, and we'd skedaddle through the aisle like wild deer. Some days we'd even play tag on the bus, and when Mama was not looking, we stuck the Spearmint gum we got from Grandpa beneath the bus seats.

Of course, there were clear unwritten rules on public transportation. Everyone knew them. The golden rule was to give up your seat if there was an elderly person, a disabled person, or an expecting mother. The best one yet—when Grandpa drives the bus, you never pay a fee or wave a pass, but instead, you give a big hug.

I wanted to ride the bus every Saturday at some point, so Mama often took us to ride Grandpa's route for hours upon hours. My experience on the bus was the highlight of my day. Grandpa was always on time as the operator of the bus, and never a minute late. The bus was at the appointed stop every fifteen minutes of the hour. Each bus stop was sparsely spread from one street corner down to every other street corner.

Grandpa was very friendly with the riders who were traveling on the bus, and yes, he became familiar with his regular passengers, too. He had Morgan Freeman's long luring narrative-style voice, non-soporific, but soothing. Some passengers would sit up close pretending to read newspapers, books, or other reading material, distracted by friendly chatter. They couldn't help themselves.

"Nice day out," they'd say. Grandpa would render the greeting of the day. "How you doin'," they'd add?

"Not too shabby, at least the sun is out. Nice day for the mall, but don't spend all your money," Grandpa would reply. The chuckles of the passengers filled the air.

"Outside is always expensive," a voice from afar would add.

"That's why I drive the bus. I could look and admire and not burn a hole in my pocket."

Route 62 became popular for destinations like Capitol Court Mall on Milwaukee's Northwest side. The mall was a straight shot from 60th Street to Grandma's and Grandpa's house on 15th North Capitol Drive, about a thirty-minute bus ride. Capitol Court was my favorite mall for the very reason that it was along Grandpa's bus route. It was the only mall that everyone could conveniently get to. Located in the heart of Milwaukee, it didn't matter who you were—you went there, you hung out there, you went school shopping there. I even spent my first paycheck at fifteen and a half there at that mall.

From a very young age, I not only learned how to ride the bus, but also, I quickly developed some street smarts, picking up social cues from the bus, mainly handshakes, signals, and other unapologetic gestures. I gained independence from riding the bus. And add self-confidence to my list—I could never get enough of feeling myself.

The nature of daily public transportation operation started at the transfer center, and from the transfer center to the numerical route assigned to each driver. The bus's headway time was every fifteen minutes at the speed that the bus moved, which was around twenty-five to thirty-five miles per hour. Every bus driver ascertained a commercial driver's license (CDL) to be able to operate a bus.

The kind of bus Grandpa drove was centrally located with many connections or transfer points for travelers. A bus pass was still valid for an additional bus ride if it was used within the allotted time (usually no more than an hour and a half if the bus driver is as nice as Grandpa). Frequent bus travelers could purchase a bus pass for under ten bucks, available at a discount fare for certain populations like students and senior citizens. You had to be assiduous though, as all sales were final, and if your bus pass expired you couldn't ride the bus. Children under six rode the bus for free with a paying adult which was always an added perk for Mama. I was a lot smaller for my age so if another operator other than Grandpa drove Route 62, Mama often lied and said I was five to avoid paying the fifty cents fare.

Somedays, I watched Mama insert a dollar into the fare box next to the driver. Once she slid the money in the slot, it sucked the dollar quickly; the money was not refundable. And, bus drivers don't give change, so she needed the exact amount required to pay for the fare. The driver handed Mama a bus transfer that listed the latest bus arrival time we could take. Then, we were free to find any available seat that we wanted, except if the bus was full of passengers. I hated standing up on the bus. I hated having to adopt a wide stance while gripping a metal pole, trying to maintain my balance on a moving bus that could either slow down or take off abruptly.

I couldn't imagine a life without the bus rides, without the mall stops, without Grandpa's hugs. I guess I'm telling you this to prove to you that I had some type of childhood. I'm telling you this because I wasn't always afraid. Some days I felt like Rudy Huxtable. I was adored.

Days weren't always still. Some days cruised at twenty-five to thirty-five miles per hour. Doors opened of opportunities. They were always on time.

AUNT DEE

I turned ten in the Spring of '91. Songs, such as "Hold On,"
"My Lovin'" and "Free Your Mind" were massive crossover
hits for a girl group, and I was the honorary group member
in my dreams. But on another note, it was the first time I
realized how my parents' breakups displaced us on many oc-
casions over the years, and how the only extended family my
sister, brother, and I had was on Dad's side. When we moved
into a shabby duplex on North 25th Street, we lived with
Dad's oldest sister Aunt Diana, but I like to call her Aunt Dee.

Mama and Aunt Dee were like two peas in a pod, although they were ex-sisters-in-law. When Mama and Dad
took a staff and parted ways like the Red Sea, the definitive
split occurred as early as when I began tying my shoes. Dad
watered his lawn livin' the single life; Mama watered hers.
Sometimes she tried to water Dad's too. It often got messy.
And there I was with my two siblings feelin' stuck in the
mud. Some days, I wish Dad would scoop us up in his arms;
we learned to settle with his sister Aunt Dee close by.

For starters, there were clear differences between my
two parents. Dad had many talents—he was athletic, and

creative, not to mention charming. You know, things any woman would want in a man. Dad paid to have all the good channels on television. We ate pizza for dinner and candy for dessert, and we drank Kool-Aid to quench our thirst. We rented movies from Nord's Video up the street from his studio apartment. More importantly, Dad gave warm hugs and sound advice for street smarts. We had a weekly allowance according to our ages—five, seven, and nine. And he was the best Santa Claus that ever crept into our tiny living room.

And then there was Mama. Mama was strict; hands down, she made the most unreasonable rules. "You can only play with two toys at a time. Put everything else away," she'd say angrily if we played too loudly. We ate tons of grits and oatmeal—I hated both. I think being a mom to Mama meant, *sacrificing my body, my time, my finances, my sleep, and my mental health to raise my kids will be worth it in the end because they will grow up to take care of me as good children do and help fill a void I have because I didn't have my own parents in my life—I just hope my kids survive my weaknesses.* She feared facing the uncertainty of the world; whereas Dad would just grab life by the balls, Mama never mastered the concept of standing on her own two feet.

When we moved in with Aunt Dee, she created a plethora of extravagant art projects, wowing us with her raw skills and talent. She stood about 5 feet 4 inches. We often admired her colorful reputation as an engaging eccentric. Aunt Dee had two children—she always compared them academically to my brother, sister, and me—and her common-law husband, who occasionally came home later covered in paint, eating grapes and cantaloupe out of the refrigerator before he washed his hands. I knew him as Uncle Marcus—the father of Aunt Dee's two children—the one she would never formally meet at the altar. But, most of all, I knew Uncle Marcus as the man who would fall asleep at random and awaken to a conversation as if he'd never checked out, amazingly picking up wherever the conversation landed. And when he snored, he roared. Never heard anything like it. We laughed. "That's not funny; your uncle has a medical condition," Aunt Dee would scold. We contained the laughter as best as eight and nine-year-olds could. But even Uncle Marcus was an artist in his own way—he skillfully and beautifully painted houses, businesses, and other large buildings, and made a decent living for himself.

I became conditioned to unconventional families, although at times, I wished I came from a "normal" family like the ones on television I fantasized about being a part of. I wanted to be Rudy Huxtable. I wanted to have breakfast, lunch, and dinner at the dining room table. My paternal grandparents were the only long-lasting married couple in my Wisconsin family. I admired my grandparent's relationship. The two were inseparable. Unlike my parents, my grandparents never separated whenever they had disagreements. Grandma would warn, "Don't worry, kids, your grandfather and I are having a discussion." My parents argued, fussed, and fought about Dad spending money and being away from home all the time—before they would eventually throw in the towel for good. Dad eventually moved out, leaving Mama to make the rent on her own, with his monthly child support payments that never seemed to be enough or the equivalent of going into labor alone three times. Aunt Dee always came to Mama's rescue just like any real big sister would.

Instead of wallowing in pain from my parents' split, I found my passion for fiber arts. While living with Aunt Dee's family, I had the vision of becoming an artist. Not only that, but Aunt Dee also made me feel extra special because she spent hours mentoring me.

Aunt Dee was tied with my paternal grandfather for being the second-best person to me—of course, Dad was the best. My paternal grandfather played the guitar, and along with Dad, also had natural talent and looks. My Aunt Dee was also artistically talented, and she would teach me to be a fiber artist, even if I had to discreetly stalk her talents while she worked. She was the first living artist I ever really knew in my life. I admired her creativity and the confidence she used to manage any tool she worked with. Aunt Dee reminded me of Picasso in the way that she abstractly played with colors, shapes, and movement within her pieces. The surrealism in her work blew me away with techniques allowing her unconscious mind to express itself countless times over. I was her silent audience subtly reaching out, my eyes applauding every manipulation made with her strong hands. Aunt Dee stood at five-foot-four and weighed about a buck seventy-five. She wore cowry beads on single braided tresses that gracefully dangled above her broad shoulders like the Williams sisters in their prime.

The rapid movement of the crochet hook in Aunt Dee's hands proved she was prowess at her skill. I watched her work looking up from the floor as she performed mini miracles with her wrists. She held her hook underhand like twirling linguini around a fork. I can still feel arthritis in her joints through each angle she made bobbing and weaving and unwinding as she prefabricated magic knots from the folds of her hands. She's magical. She's my shero. She's my favorite aunt. I love her.

The first time she peeped my interest, Aunt Dee was creating another one of her masterpieces, something new besides the personalized Afghan blankets she would traditionally make for all the children in our family. She was working on amigurumi—Japanese for a crocheted or knitted stuffed toy—a miracle webbed with a red four-millimeter hook, a ball of pretty string, and a bag of Poly-fil fiber. She introduced me to a new world of trial and error through the discovery of fiber arts.

Fiber arts and dance were the only two things I had going for me after my parents parted ways. Who needed a silver spoon when I had my own silver hook? My first hook came from Aunt Dee for Christmas the year I turned nine. It was shiny red. I carried it everywhere like a magic wand. It was the best gift I ever got besides Barbie's Dream House Dad bought my sister and me to share for Christmas the year prior. I never received anything from Mama that was noteworthy. Every year, Dad was brown Santa pulling up the night before Christmas in an old Cadillac the size of a boat, filled with gifts—everything we wished for and more.

Not only did I feel bad about not receiving gifts from Mama, but I also rarely ever felt special. One of the things that I learned from her was how to hide my secrets and sorrows behind a mask. She wore distinctive types of masks. She held up a professional mask for all my teachers during conferences, hiding her embarrassment at my below-average grades. Mama also wore a smiling mask for strangers when they complimented how disciplined and cute her three children were before they'd ask to touch our hair. What strangers really didn't know is that Mama threatened us before we entered the store: "Don't touch nothing, don't ask for nothing, because you ain't getting nothing. And if you act a fool in this store, I will beat the black off you."

Although Aunt Dee had a close bond with Mama, she really connected with my sister and me. We lived with my Aunt Dee and her two children—a boy and a girl—for quite some time, usually off and on when Mama fell on challenging times. Aunt Dee's kids never missed a meal, always had every amenity known to man, attended live concerts, enrolled in the best schools for only the gifted and talented, and yet never seemed completely satisfied with what they had. They'd often snap back at Aunt Dee whenever they were told no or given a specific task to do. They were "time-out" kids for sure. Mama would never allow us to talk back under any circumstances. Our lips would meet the back of our necks if it looked like we attempted to hum beneath our breath because children were seen and not heard.

For most of my childhood, I tried to fly under the radar, to not be noticed out of fear of doing anything wrong. *Don't you move. Don't you speak unless spoken to. Eat all your food. Don't bring home any bad news from your teachers. Cross your legs when you sit. Don't get your clothes dirty. Don't talk to strangers. And don't take anything from strangers.* Those were all Mama's commandments. I don't know if I was more afraid of Mama hitting me and pinching my ears until she drew blood because I'd broken one of her rules or of becoming Mama herself when she got angry. I learned more from the lifestyle of Mama than I did in any classroom. I guess, deep down inside, I knew what I didn't want to be. So, fiber arts became my serenity, my secret remedy for temporary joy. Fiber arts took me to places where even anxiety could not enter.

Aunt Dee coached me in her tiny living room space filled with pencil sketches on white canvas, hanging exotic African masks, and other unfinished fiber art projects. Her designs were implicit. Around the room dazzled extraordinary details of earth tones mixed with reds, blacks, and greens. We'd remove our shoes near the door whenever we entered her home. The room had hardwood flooring and a fuzzy, gray rug lay softly beneath my feet. Aunt Dee would sit in her oversized Papasan chair shaped like a sphere with a large cushion positioned inside of the bamboo frame. And then there was me, a small figure sitting crisscrossed apple sauce on the floor as Aunt Dee hovered over me to show me the slip knot.

I took a piece of rainbow-colored yarn and attempted a circle. With one end I slipped the piece through the circle I made. I inserted my hook into the circle. And I pulled both ends to tighten my slip knot. Uh-oh, it disappeared before me. Puzzled, I had no knot.

"But where did it go?" I asked.

"You lost it. That's okay that you didn't get it the first time. Try it again," Aunt Dee said.

The slip knot vanished again, only this time, I wouldn't let defeat get to me. My determination set in. It took me a few tries, but I was more eager than ever to make my slip knot stay.

"There you go, Tee."

Aunt Dee nodded as I grew closer.

"I did it, Aunt Dee."

"See. I knew you could do it. Now you're ready for your first chain."

Aunt Dee smiled back at me.

I looped and I pulled, and I looped, and I pulled some more until I had a nice long loopy lasso.

"You are a natural."

Then, Aunt Dee showed me how to build upon that nice long chain by adding a second row of chains, then a third, then a fourth, then a fifth, then a sixth, creating a block. She caressed my thick, frizzy tresses in an old hairstyle that Mama had styled days earlier as I continued to work on my rows. I could tell Aunt Dee was pleased with what I'd accomplished thus far. I often wondered why Aunt Dee never worked as closely with her own daughter as she did with me. It must have been that Marisha was never interested in arts and crafts. She learned just as I did, but Marisha never continued with fiber arts. I also wondered why Marisha wouldn't hold much interest in anything we made; her mama was so amazing at it.

Marisha's hair, miniature black braids, curled slightly under her chin into a bob-length style. She dabbled with makeup but applied it heavily, as she wanted to be noticed. Her large feet were forced into thin white fabric shoes from Payless. She carried her Walkman in hand and belched the tune to Boys II Men's "Motown Philly." While I crocheted that night she said to me, "When I get older, I'm moving to Atlanta to attend Clark University." Marisha was older than me by a measly six months. One would have thought that she was a decade older by the way she always sassed. "It's because I am the oldest grandchild," she'd say when determining who went first at anything or who oversaw all the other kids in the family. Marisha was quite hefty compared to the rest of the grandchildren. Her voice could carry an entire room. She was a daddy's girl like me, but in the absence of Dad, I clung to her mama, Aunt Dee, instead of my own. Every stitch felt like I was compulsively attacking a piece of bubble wrap. I felt in control instead of something or someone having complete control over me. I worked every day on the beginner's single stitch. Although I was a novice, it wasn't long before I started making uneven, rectangular-like shapes. The stitches I created were loose in some spaces and tightly woven in others. Suddenly, every stitch became a game of Tug-of-War. The right and left sides of my brain seemed to have minds of their own as they pulled against each other in a test of my mental strength and agility.

Maybe I was the one who was being tested or pulled from every direction, or maybe I was trying to find my natural rhythm between the lines—between staying in a child's place and being "the one in charge" when taking care of my siblings. I had to make sure my siblings didn't get into trouble and upset Mama, but I also needed my personal space to dream and create miracles like Aunt Dee. I felt like I didn't fit in anywhere because I liked to do "old people's things." I looked like the irregular shape growing from my hook. Mama expected me to be okay with the fact that she was running off with some new guy, but although I was barely ten, I recognized the face of danger. Why couldn't I be more my age and worry instead about playing in the rain, which nice shoes and matching dress to wear to school the next day, which game to play next, or which new talent would emerge?

The new guy Mama ran around with was an abuser. He was vile. He was dirty. He was shit. It was Dave. I hated the name "Dave" and the way that she said his name, dragging the "a." It reminded me of daaanger. He was a vampire whose fangs sucked the blood out of me, leaving his mark on my neck. I hated Mama. She should have known better. She should have loved herself more. She should have loved me more.

I needed a restart. I learned to frog. I wanted to face the rough patch of my life head-on and rip it.

One day, I suddenly thought of each time we moved to escape from my mother's abusive relationship with danger, in between the times we temporarily stayed with Aunt Dee, every time we changed neighborhood friends, every time we left behind something important like my Barbie Dream House—oh, how I wanted to live there, where it was pink and happy and bright. I grew weary through times of trouble. Every time the wind blew, we moved without warning, becoming one with the night. We always moved in the middle of the night when we were running, my feet getting so tired. I thought again about how much I wished I was Rudy Huxtable, always loved, always adored.

Starting all over, everything would unravel into a small pile beneath my feet like unwinding yarn. What I could pick up and fit inside of my pockets was what I'd take along with me. We moved in cadence, disappearing down the pathway to the unknown, leaving behind everything we once loved, and headed to somewhere new, in search of something Mama thought was better. Things never got better.

I felt like cheap yarn sliding through the hands of an insecure hooker who continuously made mishaps and was never sure about what to make of such yarn. I have been gathered, looped, stretched, and reused many times galore. I have been tossed, turned, and laid to the side so much that I have lost count. I've reached my limit. I've learned to trust patterns and to stay away from them, too.

It wasn't long before I got the hang of the single-stitch crochet technique. The more I watched Aunt Dee, the more I improved. I went from making odd, irregular shapes with kinks and cranks to making more recognizable, organized shapes. I was even swapping out colors, creating my own rows of sunshine and rainbows amid the clouds around me. Aunt Dee smiled every time I made progress and advanced to something new. Between the tips, tricks, and rules of crochet, she showed me how to frog and why crocheters frog.

Learning to frog was the most valuable information she could give me as a child. It was significant because I could start all over again and make every stitch better once, I ripped out all the kinks in the yarn. *If only life were that easy*—I thought. *Starting over. Ripping out a few kinks.* But I began to seek a life filled with the pleasure of joy. Joy was every time I picked up my hook to create something new that I worked on alone. Joy was sharing a large pizza and renting Blockbuster videos with Dad on the weekends. But pleasure—the pleasure was letting go of the past to find the true me.

Throughout the nuisance of trying to reinvent the wheel, I focused on what I could do versus what I could not do, and that was to make string pretty. I pieced a few things together like a scarf or two, and I even attempted my own Afghan blanket. Of course, my work missed the mark on the first few tries. Stitching was a learning process. I consistently frogged complete pieces many times over for a fresh start to emulate the things that Aunt Dee could do. I moved ambitiously without a pattern, and sometimes in over my head. I was a freethinker when creating pieces—now making perfect squares, looping perfect stitches, and creating picture-perfect patterns.

To frog meant to undo mistakes in needlework and start over again. It felt like death initially. It felt downright mortifying. My soul gasped in horror at the sight of wasted hours that would have been committed to a completed design—a masterpiece. Now a trainwreck lay crumbled inside my open casket. And after realizing how much frogging was such an important element of crocheting, I got used to it. Mistakes will happen. Pulling my hair out was not a new feeling but starting over—now that was a new feeling, a new beginning.

Throughout most of my adulthood, I have not only frogged numerous projects but also my outlook on life. My life became doable because I ignored past traumas and why some of those things continued to haunt me and hindered me from moving forward. I could frog or fold. I knew that choosing to carry all that dead weight of pain upon pain would put me in an early grave. To do that would be to accept whatever happened. But I don't always have to accept defeat. I won't.

Some days, I wished with the flick of my wrist I could frog or even fully rest on God to have a chance at a different life. A life where I never had to change homes like changing undergarments. A life where my parents made better choices, even sacrifices to save our family. A life where my parents listened to the silent cries of their children. A life where Mama wouldn't have to hide her blackened eyes.

I always wanted an older sister, so I wouldn't have to be brave enough for everyone who came after me. I wouldn't have to be the first to figure out life as Mama's oldest child. I wouldn't have to protect my younger siblings from dangerous men. I wouldn't have to be the one to "set the example" for my siblings to follow. But I am.

What is the meaning of frog to a bruised little girl, ready to rebuild upon how she felt at every moment, making sense out of madness? Finding joy. The process: Chaotic. The results: Nothing short of amazing. Strings flowed out everywhere on the floor beneath her feet, and she was like a woman in a salon chair, looking down at the hair she used to have. And as she stared into the mirror, she admired the woman staring back at her. The transformation resulted in splashes of blue, green, purple, and gold, creating a mountain of all the feelings that flooded into something more pleasurable. Although frogging meant unraveling the past and starting again—ripping it open—I knew I had to create my own second chances.

Letting my mind rest, I enjoyed the feeling that recharging would bring. And instead of the unorthodox stitches assembled into unrecognizable shapes and fragments of my imagination on the bare floor—there' hung a beautiful Afghan blanket at the end of my hook, just like the projects Aunt Dee and I used to make.

I am the recreator of my joy.

DICKHEAD DAVE

It was July, the summer before I entered the sixth grade. We no longer lived with Aunt Dee. Instead, we moved across town with Mama's boyfriend Dave. Dave and Mama pulled up in front of Lavarnway Boys & Girls Club to pick us up after a long day of swimming, shooting pool, and other recreations. We opened the door and climbed into the back seat of Dave's car. The car was small; the seats appeared charcoal colored. We sat in silence around the lingering sweet cherry scent, listening to Chubb Rock's "Treat 'em Right" ripping the radio waves. Mama looked over at Dave who was too tall, too bulky-bodied to be behind the wheel of a 1991 Dodge Neon. He kept his weasel eyes forward, which prompted Mama to stare out her window, lost in the decrepitated houses as if she were thinking about how to break out of jail. I wondered if they had been fighting about us earlier in the day. I wondered if he'd given her some type of unrealistic, utilitarian ultimatum. I wondered if he wanted Mama all to himself, to use, abuse, and discard at his disposal.

Mama shifted around in the passenger seat as we remained in position and parked for a few more minutes. We could feel that something was up. She didn't even bother to ask what we did all day inside the boys & girls club or if we'd had lunch. Dave was Dave. He never liked us anyway. His hands were still positioned on the leather steering wheel. The driver's seat was almost worn to its core, crouching, and caving into the floor. There was minimum legroom behind his seat. Sometimes Dave would purposely recline his seat all the way to the back, pinning the knees of the one who so dared to sit behind him. He made no eye contact, but his eyes were fueled with hatred. He thought it was funny to hear us squirm and scream from sore, pinned knees. I could feel the tension from the rearview mirror, although he never muttered a sound or syllable. His facial expressions were a mouthful.

Dave was Mama's appointed king of our dark castle, and we were his peasants, mere rug rats, nothing to him other than a footstool to be stepped on. For sport, Dave hunted on Saturdays alongside a Beagle he cherished, named Snoopy. When he needed props to hold the feet of the rabbits he gutted and cleaned, my siblings, and I were there shaking with all the guts, bile, and blood exposed at our feet. Mama would watch cowardly from the doorway, standing the farthest away from the carnage. Later, I never felt more guilty than eating an animal shot and skinned by a madman. It tasted like death. After dinner, when Dave demanded no dirty dishes in the sink, I'd wash them, and as his accomplice, I scrub away the blood that stained my hands.

Finally, Mama turned around in her seat nervously, the same energy as when she'd volunteered me to assist Dave in skinning the rabbit. Only, she asked the easiest question on a test that sounded like heaven's gates opening instead of the hard lyrics of Chubb Rock coming from the radio. I wondered if it killed her to say what probably tasted like garbage in her mouth. With the hasty sound in her voice, I wondered why she never asked the same question much sooner, sparing me from heartache, rather sooner than later.

"Do you guys want to go live with your dad?"

"Yes," we said.

We were excited. We started unfastening our seatbelts to hurry and flee out of the blue four-door Dodge.

"Wait," Mama said. "Are you all sure you wanna go be with your dad?"

"Yes!" we said again simultaneously.

"Tasha?"

"Yes."

"Jay-Jay?"

"Yes."

"Yes."

"I knew you would say you wanted to, Tisha." Mama folded her arms across her chest, showing off her adult-sized tantrum. "No point in asking you. You always hollering about your damn daddy. You know what? Fuck it. Go be with him. Go."

I didn't hear anything else that came out of her mouth other than the two letters "g" and "o," and I was the last person out of the car. I gently shut the door, never looking over my shoulder. Although looking back, I should have probably slammed that fucker, and let the window shatter like my heart when Mama had chosen Daaave over us like she always did. It didn't cost a thing for her to be nicer, to help with homework, to not scream a question at us when we're still confused, to not reintroduce me to a life filled with trauma and struggle. I craved hope, optimism, and joy, but all I got were scars and walls.

I heard the tires screech immediately after the door closed behind me. The smell of rubber rushed through the ratchet air. We darted across the street back inside the boys & girls club thrilled to call Dad to save the day once more.

Dad arrived swiftly. We were glad. He was pissed. He was pacing. He was sweating. He demanded answers. Answers we didn't have. We grew nervous. We climbed onto the backseat of his white Cadillac. What darkness would possess a mother to leave her three children and drive off into oblivion with some guy who was no good for anybody? *She's dead to me.* I thought to myself, *Damn her.*

I never told Dad what Dave did to me over the several months we spent with him. I didn't tell my dad how Dave was a Peeping Tom who slithered through the mirrors near my bedroom door. I didn't tell Dad about the raging red marks that stained my short, narrow neck. I didn't tell Dad about the puberty book that Dave and I'd looked at together and how I had to point to which depicted body mirrored my eleven-year-old shape. I didn't tell Dad about the dated, dark rings around my achy arms when Dave squeezed them tightly, how they were purple, black, and blue. I didn't tell Dad how Dave took my crochet blanket that Aunt Dee made me and gave it to Snoopy to urinate on. I never told Dad what Dave had done to me. I didn't want Dad to go to jail for killing Dave. I needed my dad. I loved my dad. I would protect my dad, even if that meant I would suffer.

Riding home in Dad's caddy felt just like riding Route 62 with Grandpa. I knew I was headed for a taste of life around a white picket fence. I wanted to make sure that my new journey was real. The air sounded the same as ocean waves crashing into the shore meeting sand. I let my hand stick out of my window to feel the cool air ripple between each of my fingers. I would forget about all my worries leaving my troubles behind.

Dad turned to me and asked, "Are those hickeys on the side of your neck?"

He focused his eyes back on the road and then again on me. I grabbed the left side of my neck, trying to smear the marks of shame.

"My neck is a little irritated," I said.

I felt uncomfortable lying, but something told me it would be best if I did. I put my head down for the rest of the drive home. I wondered if Dad already knew the real answer. I wondered why we remained silent on the ride. I wondered why I couldn't look him in the eye. I wondered why I felt filthy, why I felt ashamed. I wondered if Dad thought I was dirty like I did.

When we arrived at Dad's apartment, it was tiny and unprepared for three children. There was only one room, a fold-out couch, a small kitchen, and a bathroom. We slept comfortably close on the floor. The bare floor felt warm but gritty, like sand. Inside Dad's apartment was the type of safety I felt while riding on Grandpa's bus, only the smell was a lot better—Windex and fresh Pine Sol. And my only thoughts now were of no more running, and no more walls, and my scars only being the good kind from riding a bike, climbing trees, and falling down from them. Now, we'd found rest. We had Dad. Forever.

OPRAH

I loved Mama like a distant, browbeaten relative. I loved the way that Mama talked to Oprah on the television screen as if the audience depended on wandering wild wisdom. She'd hold the top of her eyelid with the tip of her thumb as if she was caressing her lashes. She'd snap, crackle, and pop sunflower seeds during commercial breaks. Then by the time Oprah returned to her studio couch glazing into the camera, Mama's voice already grew too raspy for more outbursts. She did anyway. *Mmm. Hmm. I kno dat's right.* I loved how Mama always agreed with Oprah and not with me.

I loved her bluntness, the cadence of Mama's voice, the constant guttural sounds that rattled up and down her trachea, unlike how she spoke to me brash and angry and full of profanity. The plastic bag containing Mama's soggy shattered shells, she sucked the salt off, polluting the air with a sour aroma. She'd scold my sister, brother, and me if we disrupted Oprah speaking with our daily shenanigans and horseplay. We'd much rather be playing with Barbie and Nerf guns. But she turned us into stones. We were stuck for an hour watching Mama watch the *Oprah Winfrey Show.* We waited for what seemed like hours before cracking beneath Mama's broad nostrils like her soiled sunflower seed shells.

I loved how Mama had Oprah's undivided attention and never mine. I loved Mama like I loved Oprah's soporific show topics, *How to Marry the Man or Woman of Your Choice*—I preferred Oprah watch me play. Her eyes were widely spaced across her face, just like Mama's. I wondered if we were related somehow. I wondered if I could be like Oprah someday. She's the real deal, passionate, and always pushed the envelope—the opposite of Mama. I wondered if Mama admired her as much as I did. Maybe one day we will be free from this curse.

MAURY

We met in high school. John first caught my eye in the driver's training class. I never felt that way before. He gave me chills like the kind I had after consuming an Irish Truffle Frappe. My body shivered in barely B cups. I was fifteen. He was sixteen. I was smart. He was John. I turned to meet a gentle voice from the back of the class answering all the instructor's questions correctly. He sat in the back like the bad boys do. I sat nervously nerdy at the first desk in the next row over. I leaned my shoulders back and wrapped my tresses around my fingertip four times. I wanted John to see my newly relaxed hair and how it had hang-time. My right K-Swiss swept across the barely buffed floors. Our hearts became a game of cat and mouse. I imagined my tongue taking an elevator ride down his throat. I felt my spine tingle when our eyes locked. I remembered thinking, oh God is this normal. I never knew love like this.

I wondered if our future babies would have good hair and Kool Aide smiles. I loved that he didn't have teeth like housing project windows—where some are shattered, slanted, or stained. Instead, John's teeth sparkled. Not one tooth was displaced. Mama always said nice teeth were important. She didn't want any funny-looking grandbabies. His eyes also lit the room. It was inevitable that we'd be like Carrie Brady and Austin Reed from *Days of Our Lives*. I brought him home to meet Dad. He welcomed John to our family. After high school, I followed John off into a sunny kaleidoscope over glistening blue water and majestic Hawaiian palm trees. He served in the Navy; he was stationed in Pearl Harbor, Hawaii. I left college in Wisconsin to unite with him. We were inseparable until we weren't. I wondered why my heart played tricks on me.

John and I rented our first apartment fifteen minutes away from the military installation in Honolulu. If I spun around in a circle, I could touch all the entry points meeting the pasty walls connecting the kitchen, living room, bathroom, and bedroom. Sometimes I stepped outside the front door in the kitchen to get some air. I waited for John to start my day. John came home every day of the week at 5:00 PM. Sometimes he made it home early to catch the last ten minutes of The Maury Show.

The keys rattled against the door in the next room. I also heard the doorknob turn and immediately close after. John's lean legs and black boots marched four steps from the door through the kitchen to the inside of our bedroom. He smelled like hard work and Sprite. He caught me talking to the television as I watched Maury's "shocking" lie detector test episode. I could never get enough of the audience booing. John sat beside me as I lay vertically on top of crisp light blue linen. Maury pulled out the white envelope as he looked at his studio audience and then at those of us at home watching who were unemployed, uninspired. I read aloud with Maury the not so "shocking" results of the test, "...and the lie detector test determined, that was a lie." John smirked. It wasn't funny though. Maybe the law of cheating is dummy proof; only a fool would get caught slipping.

"Would you ever cheat on me?" I asked.

"No," John said. I looked up at him. John fixed his eyes to oblivion, somewhere far from mine. He could have at least looked at me. Kissed me. Held me. Nothing. I believed him anyway. I blindly loved him just as he sat there beside me lifeless. All I could do was reassure myself that I wasn't Mama. John wasn't Dad. Then, I felt like I was the luckiest girl in the world eating pineapple ice cream from Walmart.

I thought about how Maury's lie detector test shows were more interesting than The Oprah Winfrey Show: "How to Marry the Man or Woman of Your Choice." John was my high school sweetheart; *we lived in paradise.* I thought some more. *Our love was cool like the other side of my pillow.* I wanted to play the lead role in my own fantasy.

Alternatively, our love was a sham. Our doctor determined risky behavior. John played Russian Roulette with my heart. Could it have been KY Jelly, he asked? The doctor said, "Oh no. KY Jelly won't cause Chlamydia." I could feel her discombobulation. Her eyes splattered on the floor. But for a second, I even hoped the absurdity of KY Jelly causing a sexually transmitted disease could be possible. My body was assaulted. My self-worth was in question. I didn't even need Maury to expose the truth in our marriage.

I thought about what would happen if there wasn't a cure for the spell, he put on me. His love was a revolving door. I cooked. I tidied up an empty apartment while he thought he could blow smoke back into a cigarette. He ultimately said screw our vows, I'm doing me, not you. I believed all the lies about working late, stuck in traffic, and being out with friends. I was naïve and gullible throughout three long years and two children.

I promised myself that I wouldn't waste time writing about John and me. The time I spent with John was unworthy of my time, especially being a part of such an important piece. I promised myself and the world that I would never have to waste another second conjuring up an unhealthy relationship even if it resulted in creating two of the most amazing human beings, but I did. I did it for you. I did it for the two small humans I got out of the deal. I painted them the same life-size picture that I had of a Black Superman. I did it because I was no longer that kind of strong, so strong that my heart became a metal-locked box, so strong that I became weak.

Although this isn't a love story about John and me or about how we first met, I included John. I hope it all makes sense now, how I became a wife and a mom. I hope I was still able to paint you a pretty but imperfect picture of how strongly humans value love.

I wanted my story to be about survival. I wanted my story to be about bravery. I wanted to share the wonders of the joy of being a daughter, a young mother, and somebody's prize. I wanted it to be about how I miss Dad and how I'm living without him.

Instead, my story is about popping smoke grenades to mark extraction zones in my life. Instead, my life has become about proving to myself that I'm nothing like Mama letting danger harm me as a young girl or Grandma Irma, having her motherhood swiped away, or even Grandma Lizz who led me out the front door with a stranger. Instead, my life is about me not trotting down an uneven road made for strong women, strong in their own misery. Although my life has become like a television show.

After being tired of living strong and feeling alone. I wanted to be selfish like John. Retreat.

MOTHER

I was barely legal to purchase alcohol when I donned the title of Mother. It was Fall in paradise but felt more like Spring when the sky drenched the ground. Every defilement that casually passed through Mama's family lineage sailed across the shore, then swallowed whole by tidal waves. I rebuked such shipwrecks—alcoholism, domestic violence, neglect, mental illness, and Child Protective Services snatching keiki or babies away.

Acknowledging that a curse existed in my family became the first step to ending the vicious cycle of deceit and hiding family realities. I never wanted to run from problems. I never wanted to believe in the idea that family must be a part to succeed. I never wanted to be the one who made assumptions about other mothers' parenting. "I don't know how she does it" types of mothers. What type of mom a woman becomes isn't usually something that'll be clear to her right of way. She might be the most adventurous and sweetest mother out there to outsiders. Meanwhile, her own children think she's busting the gates of hell wide open with her bad temper.

In fact, I promised myself I wouldn't be one of those mothers who gave credit to other mothers who tried their best, even though their best was never good enough. I wondered why Mama didn't opt to have a pet instead, or even a pet rock, sparing another from the steps of shattered glass. She missed the mark, the nurturing gene. If mothers do what must be done, then how come some fall short? Honestly, the only opinions that matter are the ones that come from the children, the fathers, since they're the ones most affected.

Pregnancy is not always gumdrops and rainbows, that I learned. Apparently, unconditional love is not inherent in every human, either. But I could never do Mama how she did me. Love shouldn't hurt so much. I didn't like her kind of love.

Agape love was something that I didn't understand until it was drilled into me to love anyway. Someone wronged you, love anyway. Someone hurt you, love anyway. I loved so much; I went blind.

When I was expecting my first child, I never knew I was in for a high-risk second and third trimester. However, there was zero doubt in my mind that I wasn't fully equipped to take on some challenges. I knew I wanted to be a better mom for my child, a better mom than my younger brother experienced. He always got the short end of the stick being the baby boy Mama never asked for, but a Junior Dad begged for, a baby boy who looked identical to Dad and me. Once Mama bought a large fire engine truck that flashed lights and made sounds, then she snatched it away from him, while snatching away a piece of his young soul with that truck. Mama didn't return the Cabbage Patch dolls she'd purchased for Tasha and me. In fact, we opened the box and carried the dolls out of the toy store smiling away, while Jay-Jay lingered behind with nothing. Mama said that it was fine, that boys are tough, and that he would be okay. I wanted to believe her. I pretended to believe her. I didn't see my brother cry, but in my heart, I felt each teardrop.

When I first told Mama I was pregnant, she seemed thrilled at the idea of me having a baby girl with some lines of, "I hope she has a lot of hair..." But when I met her unusual excitement— "I can't wait to dress her in pink..."—I cringed. She came across the idea of having a grandchild with more enthusiasm about femininity than anything about showering the healthy him or her love—that's what mattered most to me. She didn't like the idea of having boys. She felt that boys needed their fathers more and that they would grow up to be sissies under their mother's care. But in fact, I was thrilled when we found out we were having a boy. I was thrilled to prove the "Negative Nancy" living deep inside her wrong because she had been wrong —Jay-Jay needed his mother. Boys cry, too, even though they may not show it. They need hugs. They need kisses. They turn sweet sixteen. They attend special events like Homecoming and Prom, too. Boys need the same energy that little girls should receive from both parents.

The nurse checked my blood pressure and I thought she'd seen a ghost the way she looked just past me at the blinking screen—144/91, 151/98... I couldn't explain the sudden elevation. Maybe it was the fact that I was twenty-seven weeks gestation, and my family was on the other side of the Pacific Ocean. I waddled like a penguin onto the scale not even bothering to look at the rising numbers. It would only make my mental wars a lot worse. I already felt like Big Bertha.

I answered no to all the nurse's standard mental health checks:

"Difficulty sleeping or changes in sleeping habits?"

"No."

"Frequent anxiety or worry?"

"No." I lied.

"Inability to concentrate?"

"No."

"Irritability?"

"No." I lied again.

"Lack of enjoyment in previously enjoyable aspects of life?"

"No." This was also a lie.

"Increased appetite?"

"No". Damn, another lie. I'm hungry by the minute.

"Mood swings?"

"No."

"Negative thoughts?"

I sighed. "No."

The nurse exited. Moments later, there were three knocks at the door, and the doctor entered the examination room showing concern.

"I see that you are having a pattern of hypertension from your last three visits. Tell me, how are you feeling today?" she asked. She briskly scrubbed both her hands in the basin of water.

"I feel off," I finally said honestly. "There's tightness in my abdomen area, like kind of achy, too. My vision is blurry, my mouth is dry, and I feel weak and dizzy at times."

The doctor brushed her hands against paper towels, discarded them, and then headed for the ultrasound machine near the trash can. "Well, that sounds like fun," she smirked. I grinned. The cold gel hit me. The wand slithered across my swollen belly. *It's there.* I felt hypnotic at the vibration of a strong heartbeat. Then suddenly all the previous symptoms I thought I had faded away. Hearing the rhythmic beating was like bopping to the electric guitar. I felt it through my bones.

Later, the doctor warned me. "You may be at risk for Preeclampsia. I am going to order some labs. We also will need to collect a twenty-four-hour specimen to check for protein in your urine."

Preeclampsia is a condition that occurs in pregnant women where expectant mothers can develop high blood pressure, protein in their urine, fluid retention, and swelling. I didn't know why it was happening to me. I thought I had done everything right. At that moment, I felt cursed, I felt like the unluckiest mama bear in the world.

Fuck Preeclampsia.

Fuck this pink hospital sitting on top of a pedestal on a small island like Cinderella's castle at Magic Kingdom Park.

Fuck John for knocking me up and leaving me baring all the pain.

I thought.

Friday night, at twenty-eight weeks, four days gestation, and significantly overweight, I started seeing things that shouldn't be there—little splashes of light, fancy shapes, and colors, and suddenly images went from being magnified to floating and fading away like fog. My vision got weaker. My body's internal organs felt every pinch of pain. The tingles crept up my swollen hands, my inflated arms, and my stiff neck—and out my ringing ears. The room reeked of the peanut butter and jelly sandwich that tethered the insides of my mouth and hated it. I wondered if today would be the day that I die. I wondered if today would be the day I discovered that I wasn't cut out to be a mom. I wanted to scream but the screams shattered on the way out. I hit my call button in excruciating pain on my left side. I was in bad shape. Experiencing the ramifications of severe Preeclampsia, my body has already rejected the idea of motherhood.

John was there one minute and gone another. I was alone when the doctor and nurse entered the room. They hooked me up to a blood pressure machine which automatically checked my blood pressure every fifteen minutes. A cardiotocography (CTG) machine monitored my baby's heartbeat. Meanwhile, I was injected with the most painful jab I've ever had in my life. It contained a steroid to help my baby boy's lungs quickly develop. The experience threw me in a loop. One minute I was craving dairy and peanut butter and jelly sandwiches I don't normally eat, the next minute I'm in the operating room under bright lights and a scalpel. While the doctor performed an emergency cesarean, I felt some pressure from the tugging. I could see my husband fall to the floor. He'd seen my insides on the table and passed out. What a man. Even my childbirth was all about him. Then I felt my body shut off quick like a power switch.

The next few days were a blur. When I awakened, the pain eased up from my body as I saw the fighting face of a brave baby boy in the neonatal intensive care unit. Seeing him tangled in tubes and wearing such a tiny hat moved me. I only managed to visit him a few times a day to talk to him and just look at him. All my feelings of guilt never went away. There was the guilt of not spending enough time with him, not being able to feed him, hold him, and kiss him, and the guilt of having to give birth to him too early. He was all I needed to break every shackle, every chain from feeling like a motherless child when I was younger and sometimes even now. I'm older. We turned out fine, my siblings, and me. However, Mama is someone who I wouldn't look to for parenting or love advice. I wondered if Mama felt the same way about being a mother as I did. And if so, what changed?

Every day my baby boy fought harder, giving his all and when he finally came home, it was my joy to shower him with everything I was missing, extra hugs, and kisses. If only I was held as closely as a cell phone.

It didn't help that I married the wrong way. I didn't have Mama's vision when picking the *perfect man* to raise children with. Mama chose Dad because he came from a good home, he had both parents, and he was loved. My guy was the opposite of Dad—selfish and too immature. My guy didn't have a strong black father. My guy had a deadbeat dad instead. I was raised to fear boys and keep away from them. My guy was raised by a single Black woman, and he learned somehow to be intimidated by them as well. For John to feel strong, I had to feel weak. So, I played the role.

PART TWO

PRIVATE SECOND CLASS

In the Summer of 2007, I attended basic training as a Private Second Class. After months of begging John for a chance at finding a career, I got my one way ticket off the island. My training lasted nine intense weeks in Fort Jackson, South Carolina. The only sentimental item I carried with me in a backpack slung across my left shoulder was a family photo of me, John, and our two boys. But the family wasn't even on my mind at the moment. I was too busy thinking about what was to come in the next couple of hours, about how it was too late to turn back time. I'd given away four years of my life to Uncle Sam when I signed on the dotted line. I wondered if I'd grow to regret this decision. I wondered if I'd make it through to the end.

So, there I was, planted in a seat on a bus with a bunch of other hopeful recruits that I didn't even know. Most were younger than twenty-five, younger than me. Some were as old as forty. It wasn't like Grandpa's bus, cozy. The driver never smiled or greeted us. Instead, we'd loaded what appeared to be an old white school bus from the rear first. That was something else I needed to get used to— loading from the back of the bus. But I knew that I was in a different place, a different time, and that I'd do things that I'd never dreamed of doing before like firing a weapon and climbing walls. Our faces turned a ghastly pale as we headed through the guarded gates of Fort Jackson, down to what was called Reception.

Just that ride to Reception was a reality check for me. I had been on my own since I was eighteen, but I'd always been in familiar territory. Now, at the age of twenty-five and for the first time in a long time, my future was completely unbeknownst to me, just like it had been unknown to me in the women's shelter when I was a young girl. I went to training alone. No Mama. No Tasha. No Jay-Jay. Mama still worked at the elementary school we once attended. My sister and brother had already been to Army boot camp and were headed off to their first duty stations down in Fort Bliss, Texas. They made the big decision to swear in without me. I had no idea what to expect, except for the small details of eating three times a day in one of Tasha's letters covered in hearts and doodles, she mailed from Forward Operation Base Juarez, Iraq – we were used to eating once a day. After marriage and childbirth, joining the Army was the first real risk I had ever taken.

Before we arrived at Reception, a place where trainees go to in-process before they enter basic training, I figured we would immediately be running off the bus to shouting drill sergeants. But to my surprise, there was only one who stood there with his chest out like Macho Man Randy Savage. His large biceps rested across his chest. He appeared calm, although his voice carried like gushing water. Drill Sergeant didn't hoot or holler when he gave the briefing of the day. He didn't need to for us to receive the message. We tread lightly around Drill Sergeant. We didn't want to test his might.

The sun blinded us. We were quickly reminded how there's no heat like the Carolina heat because the Carolina heat blazed. Surprisingly, the foxes and whitetail deer stayed out during daylight hours, allowing humans to get close to them and wander around post without awareness. After all, we were squirrels in their territory.

Every day seemed chaotic. We marched everywhere. Receiving the Army uniform and field gear for the first time was like following an assembly line. Some civilian ladies never smiled that could take one look at you and tell if you were a "small" versus a "medium" or a "large" versus an "extra-large." And if you gave back talk about sizing, they'd proudly proclaim resting their hands on their saddle hips, "I've been doing this for almost twenty years, Private." We were thrown whatever size they gave us into a long green duffle bag. I walked away feeling as if I were stuffed inside of a large potato sack instead of a form-fitting uniform made for a superhero. Just to be safe, we wrote our names and the last four digits of our social security numbers on the inside of everything we were issued. Some days things came up missing, including our underwear. Laundry rooms were shared spaces. You never knew when someone else might try to claim something of yours as their own, like socks and cotton white granny panties. We would be held in reception, day zero until our drill sergeants were ready to reign terror over us in our new units in basic training.

My biggest fear in basic training wasn't Drill Sergeants or wildlife, it was doing push-ups in front of everyone. I could only do three, and the three I could do were not up to Army standards. My arms could never break the plane on the way down. It wasn't till the second to the last day in Reception that I openly did push-ups for the first time. A petite drill sergeant stood shouting in front of our four-line formation. It appeared that female drill sergeants always had something to prove. They were even meaner than their male counterparts. As new recruits, we were undisciplined. We blinked, we moved, we chattered, we wavered. With a whale in her voice, Drill Sergeant said, "Half right face. Front-leaning rest position…Move." We shifted our bodies at a forty-five-degree angle to the right, scurried into the prone push-up position, and then we beat our faces against the pavement for twenty-five repetitions. My arms hung like limp noodles. I remembered that I could barely do three correct push-ups.

"What's wrong with you, Private?" The tip of her nose and the brim of her hat hovered over me.

"I've got cramps, Drill Sergeant," I answered as I shrunk inside my misery while she looked down at me. *Pussy.*

"All the way up, all the way down. All the way up, all the way down. Now, hold it. Hold it." She paced around the entire formation of troops in the front leaning rest with her hands tied around her back. And when she felt the need to ease up on us for just a second she said, "Position of attention move."

We were upright on our feet. Chin up, chest out, shoulders back, and stomach in. The sweat continued to ease down from both sides of my forehead. My arms were previously slipping and sliding, making a soup sandwich. I thought about the light trickle that might stream down my thighs. I thought about the family I'd left behind if I was any different from Mama leaving her children for another life. I thought about Dad, how he'd say, "You gotta fight through the pain." I thought about how I would give that shrieking banshee with a mustache a piece of my mind. Add insult to injury, she wasn't even older than me.

I didn't want the smoke or to be branded as a shitbag Soldier. The only difference between her and me was that she earned a green hat that curled over on one side, a hat people feared but respected. And I was on the receiving end of the power that came from that hat. I didn't deserve to push, beat my face, or hear her howls. But in basic training, it's one for all and all for one. Everyone was accountable for any one person's actions. The smoke session until our bodies became numb to the pain only happened once in Reception.

During the remainder of the time, we were in Reception, we ate well on Thursday, Soul Food Day – slept; got jabbed with different shots; sat through long monotone welcome briefings; and we talked trash about our least favorite leadership, too. Some were better than others. More importantly, we were learning the foundations to aid us in our units in basic training.

Alas, the day came when our drill sergeants pulled up to get us. I think for the most part, many of us were anxious. Before going to training, people I knew said that life would be a lot easier if I didn't smile, laugh, cry, or get into any trouble and just maybe the drill sergeants won't notice me and I wouldn't have to worry much if I stay hidden. None of the advice mattered. Everything we did in training was part of a big game to break us down and build us up stronger.

When we pulled up in front of our unit, the drill sergeants were all lined up outside of the bus. Off to the right, our bags were identical and neatly staged (dress right dress) outside of a military vehicle. We were warmly welcomed to "I am your Daddy now!" In comparison to other military installations, Fort Jackson was the more relaxed military installation according to the Infantry guys. Relaxin' Jackson was the military base where the Army first tried to integrate genders for Basic training.

I belonged to Echo Company, 2nd Battalion 39th Infantry Regiment, also known as the "AAA-O" Battalion (Anything, Anytime, Anywhere, Bar Nothing). "Hooah," exclusively an Army thing meaning literally anything except for no. It meant "Drill Sergeant, I will do it anyway;" "Alright;" "Cool;" "Aloha;" "Stop your whining;" "Roger that;" "See ya later;" "This is some bullshit;" what to say when not sure of an answer; "It's all good," and lastly of course, "I love my fucking job."

I admit that I was pretty content, looking out of the bus window at my home away from home for the next nine weeks. That's when things took a turn. A whistle blew. I heard the words "Lodi Dodi, everybody off the bus. Move." Every green hat went from zero to one hundred. The next thing I knew, they were telling us to beat our feet. Confused, I looked down at my unbloused boots while other recruits began to shuffle and move. I followed the flushed-faced guy next to me trying not to shit brick his pants while fumbling his backpack. Drill Sergeant continued yelling and screaming at us to get off the bus and move our bags to the unit. Only the yelling and the constant nagging didn't bother me, Dad was a lot scarier than all those hats combined. All Dad had to say was, "Your ass is new mowed grass," and we'd immediately get right. Only he wouldn't otherwise harm a fly.

I learned in basic training that you never wanted to be "that guy," the example of what not to do. If you don't give them a reaction, they would move on to some other squirrel.

We each had two duffle bags of gear that we needed to haul to the unit. The unit sat towards the back of a large track and a manmade tire pit was created to fill the burn in our arms and legs. Each of our bags weighed about seventy-five pounds. I murdered my back. We were not allowed to take shortcuts to the bags, like walking on Drill Sergeant's grass. If we dared, our asses would be "new mowed grass." We weren't allowed to walk either. Every time we moved, it was with a sense of urgency. But the good thing about basic training was we always had help from our peers.

My feet failed me as I struggled to lift my last bag, the bag containing twenty-pound body armor plates. Private Fowler from Reception spotted me a few feet behind. The fog swept across her Coke bottles as she took the lead with my OD green duffle bag. The sweat made her cropped coils shimmer from each side of her patrol cap. I panted as I tried to keep up with my side of the bag. My intestines jostled against my abdomen. When we landed the bag, I felt intoxicated by the Carolina heat. I stumbled to join PVT Fowler and the remainder of the formation. I was officially known as "that guy."

We missed chow time that first night at the dining facility. We were still outdoors into the evening gathered into platoons in a circular formation. Nobody I met at reception was in my platoon. Once again, I felt alone although I sat next to PVT Fowler. She had a bad haircut shaped up like Westley Snipes's in *Blade*. She was made more for the Army than me.

We were each issued a Meal, Ready-to-Eat – an MRE. We didn't get to choose the type of meal we received. I was hoping for cheese tortellini, but I got the veggie omelet instead—which is one of the worst meals you could receive. I was sticky, sweaty, and tired; my body was covered in gravel. And when it was finally time to eat chow, I was stuck with a veggie vomelet. Drill Sergeant demonstrated to the platoon how to prepare the MRE. Anything sweet or fruity inside them was labeled as contraband. We were instructed to place all the Skittles, M&Ms, pound cakes, and other desserts in the center circle. I never wanted to eat an MRE again.

When we finally were able to lay down for bed, I couldn't stop thinking about how disgusting my first meal in training was. According to the Army, the MREs are made to withstand a parachute fall from over a thousand feet. In other words, the Army were death dealers, the meals tasted like it, too. Imagine a spongy rectangular slab of yellowish-brown barf, and somewhere in that mix, you may get some artificial specks of pickled peppers or rotten tomatoes. I remember thinking that night, I had eight more weeks of eating maggots, before thinking about missing my family, and finally drifting off to sleep.

The red phase was the first phase of my basic training life. This was where my life was under total control by my drill sergeants, and I meant every aspect of my life. They controlled what I ate and the rate at which I ate. They were my adult babysitter. There wasn't a moment in my day when I didn't see one of them. In the shower, the female drill sergeants were there to rush you out as soon as you made it under the shower. The soap lathered sparsely around my body before one of the banshees screamed a countdown from ten. The Army called them combat showers or two-minute showers. I referred to them as whore baths, just enough time to hit the hot spots: underarms, kitty-cats, and butt-cracks.

They were everywhere. They were always around. In the chow hall, the Drill Sergeant's sole purpose was to rush me to eat and make sure I didn't eat anything sweet. Fate never failed me; I always had less than five minutes from the time I picked up my tray to guzzle down my food.

On April 16, 2007, I turned twenty-six. I didn't know it then, but it would be the first of many birthdays spent away from home. Drill Sergeant Gomez or maybe his name was DS Gonzalez, approved of me having a piece of carrot cake for my birthday. I thought he was Joker. DS Gomez-Gonzalez smiled crooked a lot although he was vertically challenged. I didn't even like carrot cake that much, but on that day, it was the best cake I ever had. When I laid my head on my pillow, I remembered to thank God for DS Gomez-Gonzalez for not ordering me to knock out twenty-six or more pushups for all to see.

There were other days when no matter what the platoon did, we always got smoked (a heavy push-up session to the point of reaching mass muscle failure). For every formation, my brain was trained to be there ten minutes prior, no later, otherwise, I'd be late. It took some time to get this rule down. One day Drill Sergeant got so fed up, we had a platoon fashion show. Every fifteen minutes of the hour we were to be in a different uniform at a different appointed time in formation. Leave it to ole PVT Freeman with the square face and long legs and to fuck it all up for everybody. I called her Lurch. Her slew foot swept across the open bay where we caught very little shut-eye and combat showered, down the flight of stairs, and out the door like she had molasses stuck in her cotton briefs. Lurch never made the countdown to be in formation. It never seemed to bother her that she never made it on time either. We pushed our chests from the hot pavement in the front leaning rest position while Lurch waltzed her tired ass to the back of the formation two minutes later.

The uniform fit like an unmatched couple; it didn't have to make much sense together. Drill sergeants got really creative with corrective training. One uniform was a gray physical fitness (PT) shirt, black dress uniform shoes, green uniform socks, MOPP pants (military chemical protective suit), and a Kevlar (helmet). Drill Sergeant said we had five mikes (minutes) to get in uniform and come back downstairs and outdoors to the formation or we were getting our asses smoked. It was not a good day for any of us. But we learned a valuable lesson be in the right uniform, at the right place, at the right appointed time.

When we entered the second phase of basic training, they called it the white phase. The white phase was a big deal, a big achievement. We finally earned an hour of personal time to do what we needed to during the day. Some used this time to write letters, phone home, peacefully shower, or socialize. The white phase was the first time I ever held a weapon in my hand. I learned how to not just fire the weapon, but how to respect the weapon, disassemble and assemble the weapon, and clean the weapon. Drill Sergeant said that it's not a gun, it's a weapon, just like we weren't in the military – we were in the Army. I learned to fight differently, I learned to survive and protect myself without needing a weapon. More significantly, I learned to take a good hit to the face with a Pugil stick from PVT Fowler.

I took a lot of hits in training. The hit that hurt the most was a handwritten letter received in training. John sent me a "Dear John" letter, an ultimatum: choose your family by getting a hardship discharge or stay and be without a family. I guess I could reference the letter as being a "Dear Jane" letter. I sobbed. I screamed. I poured scorn at the audacity of him. My bunkmate gathered the scattered pages that immediately swept the floor. She read each line, apologized, then hugged me with her big bottom lip. PVT Shabazz from Alabama (she was also married) and I bonded over such a cowardly handwritten letter. The first piece of mail that I received in Basic Training was a breakup letter, the worst possible letter a Soldier could receive besides a notification of death. I thought about how he might take my kids and I would never see them again because I was stuck in basic training. A great part of me didn't want to fail, and I didn't want to quit. Why was it fair to make me choose? Why couldn't he just be happy for me, be supportive of me?

The first chance I got, I dialed home using a five-hundred-minute phone card wrapped in plastic I kept in a fabric wallet inside my left cargo pocket. I ignored the time difference between South Carolina and Honolulu. I ignored how bad I lied to Drill Sergeant to be excused to use the pay phones. I pulled my calling card out from the plastic, and I quickly pounded each key that mirrored the arrhythmia I experienced. John answered on the second ring. How classy of him. I channeled my fears through the receiver about his letter. I demanded to know why he would make a meal out of my heart and serve it to me on a platter.

"I didn't mean it," John said. "I didn't mean what I said. I was lonely. I was upset. I'm sorry." He sounded confused. I could hear the night hours of Hawaii. In my eyes John's Ohana. Ohana is family. I was so glad to hear him say he made a mistake. He wanted our family.

I believed in his sudden change of heart. I don't know why I did. But I needed to believe him. I believed in us. I couldn't get through this alone.

"How are the boys?" I asked.

"The boys are good. They are sleeping right now."

"Okay."

"I wrote you another letter explaining that I didn't mean it. You should get it soon," he said.

Before we hung up, he told me he loved me.

I didn't know which experience was the worst in basic training, the "Dear Jane" letter or the ruck marches that never ended with twenty-five pounds of gear loaded on our backs, a Kevlar, and a weapon we carried in the low ready. I have a short torso and short legs, so falling behind in a mile-long formation of foot soldiers was inevitable. The blisters that formed on the heels of my feet became exquisite relics. I soldiered on as I fought through the pain from rucking on pimple feet.

The last phase in basic training was called the blue phase. The ruck marches got longer, and the weapons training continued. We ran miles longer too. I about died. But I kept going. I didn't leave my children back home for nothing. Near the end, we tackled one of the final events where we had to crawl in the mud under barbed wire with live rounds from

M-60s fired overhead. It was then that I realized that I was no longer "that guy." When on the ground, I could see the tracers and they seemed close, but they were not really—still scary either way. My adrenaline and the natural body's response of fight-or-flight kicked in. Once I finished the course, I turned around and looked where those tracers were going, and I found that it was possible to stand up and not get hit. Those live rounds were so far above us on we slithered a hundred meters on our bellies low crawling through a mud field, obstacle, and barbwire. I was just relieved that I didn't finish last, I didn't stand, and I didn't get stuck with my head against the dirt. I made it through Basic Training without a man!

John flew in for my graduation from Army basic training. I noticed things were different when he didn't bring the boys. They remained with his mom. He came solo. He came empty-handed. No card. No flowers. No balloons. When he walked onto the parade field at graduation, he gave me a quick church hug, with his hand landing in the middle of my back. We didn't fully embrace, like lifetime lovers, we were instead business partners raising two boys. Our interaction was just as dry as a corps.

I knew immediately it was someone else. It was over in his eyes. The way he stood disconnected and staring into space when I introduced him to my peers. That had to explain the letter he didn't mean to send. We should have ended with the letter. His showing up to South Carolina was more about him, than me, to probably see if I was really what he wanted, to screw me one last time.

He was somehow different now. I couldn't pinpoint it. He went for a goatee. He's no longer the clean-shaven that I once knew. His love was now a brick wall. I heard the birds chirping, while I accomplished one of the biggest things I ever accomplished in my life. Maybe he had someone else to celebrate at home – that's the answer to the riddle. He didn't write often. Our conversations were flat-lined, they needed reviving. I bet he found someone new who is the opposite of me. Someone thinner. Someone half white like the girls he cheated on me with. Someone who didn't mind coming second to his mother.

He didn't have the guts to face me. He called me on my cellphone. "It's not you. It's me. I want out." John said. He promised it was no one else, he was just unhappy, but I knew better. My happiness wasn't his kind of happiness. My love was patient and kind. When basic training ended, so did we.

John told everyone back home in Wisconsin that I left him with two boys. I'm sure he got sympathy votes from mutual friends. I needed to be the villain in our story. I was his Cruella Deville, and he was a lost dog. The truth might as well have been somewhere in between.

My truth is, I left home because I was missing purpose. I thought I would find it somewhere else. Perhaps someone would give it to me. Instead, I found the soldier in me along the way amid violet smoke.

BLACK SUPERMAN

The Superman I knew and loved had skin like the fire-gold glow of the Sahara Desert. I called him Dad for short. Over the years, he breezed through chemotherapy, dialysis, heart surgery, brain surgery, then more rounds of chemo faster than the speed of lighting until that May before the pandemic hit worldwide news when kryptonite rendered him powerless. He died fatigued in a twin bed in a cold hospital room in Wisconsin, surrounded by family who bickered like strangers. The nurses draped an airy white blanket over his untrimmed toenails that had curled over the skin. After fifty-five years, it was his time to pop smoke. He shrunk ten times his size the day he died. He no longer held up the same silky sky, shooting bright comets from his eyes and illuminating my world with pretty pastel pinks and purples. He was no longer the man of steel who had the incredible power to become invincible, to see through walls, and carry me away from any fear of present danger. I watched his soul leave his body and vanish through white smoke.

I should have had more time.

I wish I had more time.

I needed more time.

The world needs great black dads.

I cried to myself when he died, hoping my soul would listen and soothe away my tears of doom that felt like acid, burning as each tear smeared a face of despair. "You gotta fight through the pain," my dad always said when asked about treatments and procedures. "Fight" and "pain," were one of the same for me. It's a hard thing to do, especially when you are always the one who others look to as "so strong."

He just lay there, his colossal being, illuminated by the entrance of heaven's gates. I felt the weight of my heart longing for my giant hero, as life as I knew it slowly slipped away. Dad had a brief life. To say that I wish it was much longer would subject him to even more pain. "I'm okay, Dad if you have to go," I lied. After all, he was only being "so strong" for his family. Letting go was the best strength I could give back to him.

I spent a lot of time away from home serving in the Army. That is something I will always regret. I never really felt in tune with things occurring back home. I missed out on all of Dad's appointments. So, I tried to relish every moment I had with him when I came home on military leave, however brief the visits could be. There was one visit near the end when we discussed movies for most of the day. Movies were our thing.

"Did you see *Prometheus*?" Dad asked. He seemed pleased with his taste in horror movies.

"Yea, I saw it. It wasn't that bad," I said. "But it wasn't that good either, Dad."

"I thought it was pretty good. You know it's the sequel to *Alien: Covenant*?" Dad sprinkled his Newport onto his porcelain antique ashtray next to his side of the couch. He tried to be considerate of my allergies to cigarette smoke by blowing the smoke the opposite way of me, but the tips of my nostrils felt like a bee sting.

"Hmm." He did not change my mind. I was surprised by how much he approved of the movie. It wasn't zombies ripping flesh.

"You seen *Aliens*, right?"

"Yeah, I saw all of 'em. And I loved all the Alien movies. I even watch 'em whenever they come on cable. But I could barely see what was happening in *Prometheus*; the movie was just too damn dark."

"What kind of TV y'all got?" Dad asked. He took the last puff on his soggy cigarette and then smashed it onto the white porcelain. I got a glimpse of his powdered knuckles and long fingernails before he reached for the remote.

"We got a Vizio, but it ain't like yours. Yours shows the picture clearer." I complimented both Dad's seventy-inch television screen sitting right in front of us – a big TV for a big man who knew good quality. He recognized the *good* shit.

He started flipping through the TV channels to find something good for us to watch. As usual during the afternoon, ain't nothing worth watching but *Maury* or *Jerry Springer*. I glanced over at Dad; he looked fragile. I thought about the last time he'd had anything other than a cigarette and a Pepsi. Then, I thought about bringing everyone

together—like we always do—before I headed back to Fort
Eustis. Every time I visit, my five other siblings and nieces
and nephews got together for a night with Dad, and we'd
have dinner and a movie.

"Should we order Balistreri's?" I asked.

"Yeah. I could go for some Balistreri's," Dad said. I could
hear the excitement rumble in his gut.

"Balisteri's pizza is the *good* shit, but I sure miss Ned's
pizza," I said. "We grew up on Ned's. Remember that, Dad?"

"Yeah. Over on 55th Street when we used to rent movies
from Nord's." Dad seemed to struggle to recall.

"They had all the *good* shit. You let us pick out whatever
scary movie we wanted to watch."

I sure missed the days when you could judge a good
scary movie by its cover and the font style of the title, movies with red aggressive letters like the cover of *Killer Clowns
from Outer Space*. Dad continued to scroll through the channels. Damn. We missed *Maury*. No *Jerry*. There's nothing
on, I thought. An awkward silence filled the room. Neither
one of us wanted to address the real elephant in the room:
his health.

"You look good, Dad," I finally said. "Looks like you lost
some weight."

"Yeah – I lost thirty-five pounds. The doctor said I needed to lose some weight before I had my last surgery. And
now I'm down to 185."

"That's good shit, Dad."

"Yeah, you know, doctors trynna get this TTP under
control, you know. Every five years or so, *it* flairs up."

He took a long pause followed by a hard sigh. Dad had
learned of his TTP diagnosis at thirty-three years young.

He had bad blood that clotted too often. "Next time *it* happens though, *it*'s gone be bad, *real* bad," Dad said matter-of-factly. He nodded his head confirming real certainty but didn't look at me. We called the stroke *it*—every time he had one, *it* outdid the last one like *it* was a competition or something.

I was too afraid to ask for clarification of *it*. He had already had a few strokes behind his Thrombotic Thrombocytopenic Purpura. How bad is *real* bad? During his last stroke, he was driving on the wrong side of the road. Now that was *real* bad. Thank God for Good Samaritans. It was frightening, you know. He was just driving down the road not too far from the house when *it* happened. *It* came out of nowhere. I closed my eyes for three seconds, trying not to let Dad see a tear seep through.

"Dad, let's watch *Dawn of the Dead* when we order Balistreri's," I said. He agreed.

If only Dad had given up smoking a long time ago. I was twelve when I first requested that he stop. I saw the damage that smoking could do from TV commercials and from reading school pamphlets the teacher sent us home with, shoving them into our backpacks as we darted towards the school buses at the sound of the bell. There was always someone else's father and sometimes mother on the front cover with a hole in the middle of their throats. These pamphlets advertised the smoking victims singing their should-of-could-of-would-of's. And, when public handouts didn't seem to appease the avid smoker, they'd conjure up fancy numbers—over 480,000 Americans meet their demise each year from smoking cigarettes, the researchers say. But, I thought, Dad could never be a part of those statistics; he dodges bullets, sees through things, and he doesn't inhale the smoke.

But coming home at age twelve with anti-smoking pamphlets inside of my backpacks became an afternoon ritual. I wouldn't be telling the truth if I didn't say how much I secretly enjoyed seeing Dad squirm from more and more "propaganda" each day – the way he raised his eyebrows, confusing the smoking pamphlets for an important letter requiring his signature like he expected a permission slip for a field trip instead. As I turned to walk away, I could feel Dad grinning as he carelessly tossed them off to the side. It wasn't before long that the pile heightened. The smoking brochures ended with baskets landing center mass inside of the trash can and me being annoyed.

And even when Dad went to the bathroom, we'd have a surprise pamphlet waiting for him on top of the porcelain toilet seat. Waiting for his bladder to get full felt like an eternity. I could hear the toilet flush, then spin, then wail, and seconds later the gushing sound of the water flowed from the sink's faucet, then there was utter silence.

I could hear Dad's footsteps. He was coming quickly. The door sprung open. Dad yelled, "Y'all gonna stop puttin' this shit in the bathroom." Dad grew serious. My brother, sister, and I became nervous.

"I'm not gonna quit smoking," Dad said.

We stared up at him from the couch. And, suddenly, the lines on Dad's forehead disappeared. Dad became Dad again. His mood lightened, so we giggled.

He's not mad at us. Good. I sighed.

Today, PSAs against cigarette smoking are more creatively enticing. They look much like the start of horror movies before they deceive their viewers with the ramifications of smoking cigarettes. However, the most terrifying anti-smoking advertisement on TV could conjure did not seem too convincing or real enough for Dad.

Before the first time Dad got sick, he worked one job, got off, and then worked at another similar job, all like routine clockwork. He helped people, senior citizens living in group homes with mild to severe mental and intellectual disabilities. Dad had come a long way from flipping burgers and collecting aluminum cans for spare cash.

Late one evening when I was fourteen, my siblings and I were at home with our stepmother. We'd had Cousin's sub sandwiches for dinner, and I was brushing the taste of onions off my teeth, preparing for school the next day.

Our stepmother, Necola, broke the news to us lightly. "Your dad fell at work. He's in the hospital. In the morning, I'm going back to Saint Joseph's Hospital. Did you guys want to visit your dad, or did you guys want to go to school?"

Miss school? I loved school. It was my outlet, my safe space. I didn't know what to decide. I hated hospitals.

"I want to go to the hospital," each of my siblings responded.

"Okay, I will let your dad know," our stepmother said. "Tisha, did you want to go to school tomorrow?"

"Yes, I'm gonna go to school," I said. Without looking up at her, I became quickly disconnected.

I thought nothing of Dad's fall the remainder of the evening. Some days heroes fall, and they get back up and become even stronger and that's that. After all, my stepmother seemed okay. And Dad was strong. He didn't need me there.

Instead, he needed me to get good grades during my freshman year of high school.

I went to sleep that night on my usual nice pallet, spread onto the living room floor. Only sleep did not come easy for me. I became restless. I tossed and turned and rolled around until there were only two hours remaining before it was time to head off for the school bus I would never catch.

I missed school the following morning based on a hunch of uncertainty. I decided to go to the hospital with my siblings instead. When we arrived, there was Dad sitting up in the bed, wearing a hospital gown, only he didn't look sick. He looked optimistic.

"Hey, I thought you were going to school." He looked at me and seemed delightfully surprised.

"I changed my mind."

We hugged. I planted him a peck on the cheek. I examined Dad lying in the hospital bed. I didn't see any casts or signs of broken bones or missing limbs. It appeared only that he'd fallen, and that the doctors had monitored him at the hospital. The one thing I found out of the ordinary besides Dad not being at home was his tray of barely touched baked chicken, mixed veggies, and mashed potatoes, sitting off to the side, now cold. I bet it tasted like paper.

It was 8:00 AM, and I was sitting on a stool in a hospital room at Saint Joseph Hospital, instead of in the first period. Normally, I had Art Foundations with Ms. Payne. Ms. Payne was so old that she was also Dad's high school art teacher too. He called her Ms. Payne in the Membrane. Only an art or music teacher would continue to rock such a mullet. Three knocks at the door and a woman in green scrubs entered the room, peering over Dad to take necessary vitals. "What is your pain level on a scale from one to ten with ten being the highest?" she asked.

Dad responded, "About a four or five." This is a scene I had observed frequently on television but had never actually witnessed at a hospital. To watch my dad lying there hooked up to the beeping machines seemed surreal—watching the lines on the monitor while listening to its rhythmic sounds, knowing that Dad was injured, that I was observing what might be the pivotal moment that changes our lives forever.

For three more nights, we continued our daily living without our dad. We ate dinner without him. Discharge day came and went. Dad was finally home, and everything seemed to be back to normal. It appeared as if nothing ever happened until it did. Because then, Dad broke the *real* news.

"I had a stroke," Dad randomly blurted out one day.

He sat forward on the stiff couch in the living room, both hands hanging lifeless in his lap.

"One side of my body couldn't move, but I could see the door. I struggled to open the door to the bathroom. I don't know how I got it open after fighting with the knob. But as soon as I opened the door, I fell forward. One of my co-workers found me on the floor."

We sat there in the living room with our jaws dropped in disbelief, listening to Dad's near-death experience, chills crawling down our shoulders. But he didn't die. That was the first time my dad became invincible like Superman.

After all, even when suffering from illnesses, Dad never complained. Never. Not even once. Instead, he focused on leaving lasting impressions on everyone who loved him. I longed for him. Whenever I was in trouble, Superman was to the rescue. But he loved his smokes like he loved his Pepsi. Why is everything we love worth dying for?

I remember thinking about that the last time we both sat on the couch making small talk watching *The Wire*. Dad loved *The Wire*. I wasn't really a fan of prison shows, so I passed the time by telling him about my better days overseas. I never discussed the hard days, the close calls in Iraq. Instead, we talked a lot about Kuwait, about what it looked like over there. Something safe Dad would understand. Kuwait was peaceful. Kuwait was fun. Kuwait was the last safe zone before we entered Iraq. All the soldiers were processed through Kuwait.

"What does it look like over there?" Dad asked as he grabbed another cigarette to light.

"We arrived at night, so I couldn't see much of the city outside of the compound," I said. "I only saw the outline of the architecture and well-lit multi-lane roads, and I also saw a few nice cars on the road on the way to the base. You know camels in Kuwait always have the right of way and if you hit one, you bought it."

Dad had never been outside of Milwaukee except to attend my uncle Tyrone's funeral down in California. It took the death of his brother to step foot on a plane. When I turned twenty-one at the beginning of 2001, we were stationed in Hawaii. I couldn't get Dad on the plane, even though he always wanted to vacation there.

"When I think of Kuwait, I think of dry desert land, camels, and flies," I said with a sigh.

Dad nodded. He probably thought the same. But really, the sky in Kuwait is very serene at night, like staring at an oversized oil pastel canvas of Van Gough's *Starry Night*.

We lived in large, oversized tents and slept on cots inside of OD green military-issued sleeping bags. We used Porta Johns when our bladders became full, which often smelled as bad as smoke pits, or designated smoking areas, maybe even worse. To deal with the stench, I learned to hold my breath frequently for long periods of time. It was like wading underwater, trying not to drown.

"You remember the movie Friday After Next?" I asked him.

"Yeah." We smiled as he waited for how I would reference the movie.

"Well, they had a place called Holy Donuts on the military base."

"Get out of here." Dad chuckled.

I quoted Mike Epps's character when Day-Day rhythmically chants, "Ho-ly-Mo-ly-Do-nut-Shop." I told Dad how, when we approached the register to purchase donuts, the Kuwaiti took our order, and I requested, "Can we get a dozen donuts, and please hold the flies?"

Dad laughed out loud. I snorted. Then we both laughed until our stomachs became weak. We were happy at the moment. I only wished that these moments, or even I, were enough for Dad to stop smoking for good. But they weren't, and I wasn't either.

I guess self-annihilation included taking risks. Even Superman took risks. I used to feel extreme guilt and self-blame for Dad's smoking days. I do not feel that way anymore. Instead, I feel a void. He made his choice. Now I am living with it. Barely.

1991. Before Dad had his first stroke, I quickly learned the meaning behind "curiosity killed the cat" when I tried a puff of cigarette tip left inside Dad's ashtray. I don't know why I did it. But I did it. Before I took on a real cigarette, I pretended to smoke a lot because I thought it was cool to do, to mimic adults. I graduated from the fake cigarette candies we purchased from the corner stores for fifteen cents a box to Dad's leftovers in an ashtray. Only the real thing was nothing sweet and chalky, like candy. It tasted like death.

I lit the cig with Dad's lighter. My eyes watered like a garden hose, and I coughed many times. I got really dizzy, and I felt like vomiting everywhere. I felt weird, like really, really weird, in a way that I have never felt before. I coughed all the way through the cigarette. When my siblings asked me what I thought about it, I said to them, "It's okay," but I said to myself, I'm never doing this shit again.

Taken back by the experience, I took a swig out of Dad's soda can. The Pepsi was flat from sitting out, untouched. I never touched another cigarette again—not even at the request of Dad to hand over a pack of smokes from the top of his dresser, and not even when I entered the Army, surrounded by many service members who smoked like champs.

1999. I watched classmates drop out of school because of teenage pregnancy, and I watched others go about the fast life, selling street drugs, mainly. I later figured out that the key to having some sort of life was to watch the mistakes other people made and not make them. Simple. What role models? I had none in real life, only on TV. My parents raised me using fear tactics, but the fear of dying from smoking never phased them. And fear never prepared me for anything. Instead, it crippled me because I relied on my friends to tell me what they'd heard other friends tell them about smoking, drinking, and premarital sex. As little as I knew about everything my friends were doing, I kept my promise—I would never pick up another cigarette again. Only everyone I knew smoked. It was hard to stay away from it. It was cool to smoke, to be part of an in-group. And I guess I was never part of an in-group. I belonged nowhere. However, I kept my oath. I never smoked.

I found out that life is all about making money to survive. At least, that was one thing I learned from my dad. Throughout my life, I have done what my dad was good at. He was a hard worker. He worked long hours. He provided. I was a sales associate at many retail stores. I worked at Taco Bell for my first semester in college. At twenty-one years old, I was a Navy wife and a stay-at-home mom living in Hawaii. I have experienced postpartum depression. As a soldier, I experienced combat in both Iraq and Afghanistan. After military service, I was a substitute teacher. I was a daughter broken into pieces by the declining health of her father. And now I am a daughter who misses her father after he is gone. That experience has given me strength like nothing I could have ever trained for in combat. Grieving Dad felt like a rollercoaster I could never stop riding.

And even so, I never smoked.

If I were to ever pick up the habit of smoking, during my third deployment would have been the time. I was beyond stressed. The Sergeant First Class that oversaw the Brigade's admin office was a nuisance. I did nothing right the first time around. And there was always work that needed to get done without a moment's pause. He kept a tight rein on the office, leaving any sign of morale non-existing. The thing that saved me from smoking a pack a day during that deployment was the fact that there was no one in my office

I could share a smoke with. Every day between the hours of 1300 to 1530, the alarm would sound of INCOMING. INCOMING. INCOMING. SEEK SHELTER. SEEK SHELTER. The announcement was followed by a piercing sound that stopped me dead in my tracks. I grew fatigued from running. I grew fatigued from carrying an M16, from which I never shot a single round. I grew fatigued of man-made bunkers surrounded by concrete T-walls and sandbags busting from the seams.

Leaving Dad's house, the world presented itself as raw. I became used to the idea that most people were smokers. I learned to tolerate the distinct aromas of cigarettes, not just Newport Menthols but Camels, Salems, Marlboro, and Winstons. Even though the smoke made my eyes water, I learned to accept the reality that some friends smoked. For ten years, I served in the Army. And I think I have breathed in about every variety of cigarette brands just by standing next to different people in military formations. The smokers I knew were like zombies in the way they hunched over as they walked to the designated smoking area every hour on the hour for a ten-minute break they couldn't function without.

2007. I was an Army Private. I had a small circle of friends, and only one of them smoked; she dipped. I thought it was the most unorthodox thing in the world for a lady to do. She was a short, nice woman who'd joined the military in her early forties. Life had already hit her hard. We bonded over our love for the islands, and we often exchanged the "hang loose" gesture in passing. She was an islander, originally from Palo, and very laid back. She had olive skin, and her left cheek protruded like Popeye's. She carried a spit bottle in the cargo pocket of her fatigues. Her real name was Nigrutang or something like that. We called her NG for short because no one could pronounce it.

"Why do you do that?" I asked one day about her dipping habit. "It's not lady-like."

"Well, I'm not a lady; I'm a soldier," NG said.

Our fists dapped. We knew that to fit in and advance within the ranks of the military, we must let go of any femininity in the workplace. She was always one of the guys. She boasted about the Army paying for teeth whitening for soldiers with stained teeth who smoked or used snuff. I'd never seen NG's teeth so white after she got it done. And what a difference it made. Only, the whiteness lasted for about a week before she started dipping again.

"Soon, teeth whitening won't matter, and you will be without teeth," I told her.

"Don't worry... I'm gonna quit... one day." NG smiled.

We parted ways. NG joined the others in the designated smoking area known as the smoke pit. I headed over to the end-of-day formation early. I thought more about Dad, about the times he said he would never quit smoking. I wondered if smoking ever got as old as the way it lingered in the air.

2018. After the Army stationed me on Fort Eustis for four years, my career ended early; I was medically retired. I headed over to the Soldier Support Building, Room 116, to receive my completed DD-214. When I finally got it in hand, it was like reading my report card. It captured everything I accomplished while serving.

I entered the room to find a pale woman, who met my eyes with a pleasant smile. She had the teeth of a smoker. She was nice, I could tell. Her hair was like a halo on her head. A small, fragile lady with tiny ankles and high heels, Ms. Crane was tucked inside of her cubicle, holding my freedom papers in her hands—everyone understood your ass belonged to Uncle Sam. "Here is your American flag and your nice certificate," she said as she presented me with a fancy cardboard box labeled "Soldier for Life." I loved the irony of being a soldier for life, by the way. "Congratulations! And thank you for your service," she added.

Ms. Crane wore her glasses on the brim of her nose. Dozens of posters displaying various animals were plastered on the wall behind her. I grasped that she probably lived alone, owned many cats, and was very liberal at heart. Although I could be dead wrong.

My facial expression did all the communication when receiving my retirement certificate. Ms. Crane must have caught wind of how my smile transformed into a disappointed frown. I skimmed through the verbiage straight down to the bottom right-hand corner of my certificate. "I know you probably don't care for the person who signed it." She pointed at the name of the former president.

And she was right. What a stain! As soon as I left the office, I went straight to my car where I began to tear up. Not because of the smear on my certificate but because starting over felt unnerving. I felt that little butterfly feeling you get wiggling inside of your gut. All I knew was that it had been ten years since I could live how I wanted to without anyone telling me what to do, when to do it, and how to look while doing it. I immediately thought back to ten years ago in basic training the first time I phoned home to speak with Dad. I was nervous I wouldn't graduate.

"Dad," I'd said. "I'm not gonna make it. I don't think I can do it." I never thought of myself as physically strong, never having had upper body strength. Hearing, "You can make it" in response from him sounded simple, but it also meant the world that he saw me as someone larger than myself.

It turned out that there was a lot I had to get used to from serving in the military, and suddenly, I was retiring early due to a battle with my mental health. And that was the scary part of it all. Receiving my DD-214, a folded American Flag in some fancy cardboard box, and a retirement certificate signed by 45 was only the beginning.

My military career and all the glory it once entailed were over. Even as I prepared for the last farewell and the emotional goodbyes with my stomach all twisted and tied in knots as butterflies. I knew it would not be long before my replacement moved in. The military service moved on quickly. My desk was not fully cleared for long before the new position immediately filled it back up.

I'm done, I said inside of my head. Walking back to the car with my hands full of memories was the longest walk ever. Mind-boggling. What would be my next move? No more showing up to places ten minutes early—whenever I showed up on time, they met me with, you're late! No more stench of smoker's breath in accountability military formations. No more acrid smells of death coming from military uniforms. No more soldiering and pairing up with NG's recycled bad breath and stained teeth. And the good news was that retiring left me to find my complete self again. No longer lost in a world of fully confined space but loved the fact that I could go home freely, anytime I wanted to, to visit Dad, to build the fondest memories without restrictions.

There I was, behind the wheel of my minivan, not looking back. Just like that, life came rolling along. And so did the Army in my rearview mirror.

I thought long and hard about when I was a kid once I got on the road to see Dad. When I grew up, Dad and my stepmother puffed and passed Newport Menthols like trains in Grand Central Station. They lit cigarettes in the morning and afternoon, and they fired up again at night, sometimes going through a pack or more a day. They even smoked on the toilet, cracking a window to let in the fresh air. They were heavy smokers, habitual smokers, and faithful smokers, too. The offensive smell of Newport Menthols pierced my eyes together like staples. The nicotine made my nostrils want to scurry away to the back of my head and down my spine. They smoked through all the lectures and carefully placed pamphlets on the nightstands that harped on how smoking was hazardous, and how smoking killed.

While driving home, I also thought about how Dad always found some humor in my siblings' and my persistence to put an end to his smoking for good. We lectured him about the effects of smoking as if he didn't already know.

"Daaad! People who smoke suffer from bad breath, and stained teeth."

He laughed.

"Daaad! Your lungs are crispy like bacon."

He laughed.

"Daaad! You're gonna talk with a microphone to your throat."

He rebuked. "I don't inhale! They do not know what the hell they are talkin' 'bout."

With a flick of his wrist, he'd dismiss any talk of smoking television infomercials. After a while, our efforts ceased with no luck of Dad ever quitting. There was no use in beating a dead horse, so we drove on.

When my sister and my brother became of age, they too became frequent smokers. Their weapon of choice – Newport Menthols, even after all the trouble we went through as children protesting our no-smoking campaigns. They both began smoking, serving in the military with other smokers. My sister Tasha started smoking while stationed in Korea. It started as a social thing. Even after all the exertion spent campaigning as kids, smoking was the one topic where any logic seemed to have vanished like a ghost.

I admit it; I looked at Tasha a little bit differently when she smoked. She reminded me of a withered rose, where inhaling the fragrance brought me disintegrating pleasure.

"It's psychological," she warned. I didn't get it. I frowned. She added, "You tell yourself, I'm stressed; I need a cigarette. I ate a meal; I need a cigarette. It calms you down; it relaxes you."

"I can't relate." I shrugged.

"Well, it's like with any addiction. It just becomes incorporated in your day, and it becomes a habit," my sister lectured me. By this time, Tasha had become a little annoyed with me. Meanwhile, I was wondering where all logic went—smoking kills. Knowing what smoking can do, why would she even do it?

Dad's father, our grandfather, also smoked Newport Menthols a lot when we were kids. He'd keep them in his front breast pocket. For years, Grandpa smoked until his heart went bad. He came out of the hospital with a brand-new mechanical heart instead of an actual healthy pumping heart. Since then, Grandpa has quit smoking. I think he was afraid that, if his pacemaker stopped working, he'd meet his doom. Grandpa understood the effects of smoking. He made lifestyle changes.

The paradigm was too simple – smoking equals death. Everyone chooses their own destiny. I see smoking as a way to self-annihilate. I wish that choosing to quit were as simple as Smokey the Bear's motto, "Only you can prevent forest fires!" But it never is—easy, that is. The tune is more like a broken record.

It didn't help that Dad was a twenty-ton block of cement for hospitals and appointments. Like a mule, once his mind was all made-up, he was always going to do what he wanted. I used to think Dad was a very good liar, but really, how fair was that? We were all only pretending not to see what was presented right before our eyes. We knew about the frequent dialysis appointments, scheduled surgeries, and continued visits to his primary care provider and specialty care doctors and the tray of add-on medications Dad had to take daily, but no one ever mentioned any of that. Maybe the family thought like me—well, he's Superman. He could hold the weight of the world. But even strong people need someone to lean on. And I wish I'd been more persistent with facing the hard truth—we wouldn't have long with Dad.

When we talked over the phone, Dad would talk about how everyone else was doing. "You know your sister, Tiffani is engaged," he boasted. I never met the last guy.

"Yeah, that's good, Dad, but how are you doing?"

"I'm doing good."

"Hmmm…k…well, I will be home in August to come see you," I said.

"I can't wait," Dad said. And I thought, me neither, because then I could see with my own two eyes if everything was really as good as he suggested.

I had not seen any part of my father's body other than his hands and face and feet—he is missing a toe from gangrene. I suppose I am thankful for the jackets, jeans, sneakers, and baseball hats that he wore even inside the house watching TV—the added layers really disguised many of the clues of changes in his health. I was afraid to learn what his body looked like from the inside out.

When I hugged him, I got an epiphany. When I hugged him, I knew I shouldn't let go because, when I did, he would soon wither away, and I would only be left with pieces of him—an urn on a silver roped necklace that I would wear every day.

2019. I saw Dad for the final time. I'd been out of the service for a year when the medical staff admitted him into Froedtert Hospital. The doctors and nurses seemed to talk in circles and offered a lot of nothing but ice chips, pillows, Ivs, and broth. Dad was almost unrecognizable at that point. If I touched him, I feared he might fade away like the ashes he flicked out the window, meeting the fate of the wind.

Out of nowhere, the doctor greeted the family with the bad news people only get in either movies or nightmares: "He doesn't have long. The only thing we can do is keep him comfortable." The moment was surreal. Everything went dark. Saying goodbye wouldn't be easy. I'd known for years that we practiced it daily, at the end of the road. We'd hug. We'd kiss each other on the cheeks. We'd share lines of, *See you soon. Drive safely on the road*. And of those times when I came to visit Dad, I always expected that I would see him again, never thinking that it would be the last good-bye. I took time for granted. I took his power for granted. Acknowledging that day as the last time I would ever see Dad again or hear him speak about the latest horror movie worth seeing was unimaginable. I could not fathom a day leaving his side that we may never see one another again. When I think about that ultimate day with him, my heart breaks all over again.

I often imagine what I would have said differently to him if I had known how little time we had. How would I address the elephant in the room? Would telling him for the last time that I hated how he chain-smoked cigarettes upset him or hurt him in any way? Maybe I would have said to him that I recall the smell on everything, in everything, through every-thing—that feeling of toxins creeping into the lungs. Maybe I would have said to him that it was all his fault.

I wish I could have brought him all-you-can-eat but-tered hotcakes with maple syrup. As a kid, Dad used to have breakfast nights for dinner. I wish we could have had breakfast.

At least a dozen times that final week, we planned his coming-home party from the hospital. A party we would eventually have carried out without him, in his honor. There was old-school hip-hop and rhythm and blues playing in the background. We enjoyed pizza from his favorite Italian takeout restaurant, Balistreri's.

We took turns sharing our memories of him. When it became my turn, I asked my siblings if they remembered the time riding in the back seat of Dad's Cadillac. We had started bickering over something stupid. Dad grew tired of us arguing, but we ignored his complaints and threats to get us to stop fussing. Dad got so mad that he pulled over at a stop sign. He made all of us get out of the vehicle, stand in a circle, and hold hands. We were so embarrassed as the other cars continued to drive around us. Maybe they were wondering why these kids were on the side of the road in a circle like a cult where dad was our infamous leader, warning us not to say another word when we got back inside of the car or else, we would have hell to pay. Maybe having obnoxious little brats contributed to our dad's smoking habit. But, as long as I'd known him, he had smoked.

I spotted his ashtray on his side of the couch as we continued to share fond memories. It was on the side of the couch that he always sat on with a perfect view of the television. The space was just how he'd left it. In fact, it was as if he had just gotten up to use the bathroom. It felt like he was due back at any moment. I held on to that moment as long as I could. The smell of smoke came through the room.

The Spring after cancer webbed his brain, lungs, kidneys, and intestines, spreading like a spider web. I thought about Dad and the state he would be in if he were alive during COVID-19. We were living in different times. Since I relied on the premise that God established our steps, not us, I reassured myself that this place we called heaven came at the right time for Dad—he'd had so many preexisting conditions. I do not know which would have been worse, dying of lung cancer or COVID-19, or both. I trusted that everything that happened, happened for a reason.

One day that spring, I sat in a full classroom at work near the back windows. Our employer briefed us on the ins and outs of teleworking from home because of the severity of this global pandemic. People were afraid of exposure to illness, but fear never lived in me. And, if I had Dad's genes, I, too, was invincible through the worst of it all – at least, for a while.

But masks became the new normal. Toilet paper and hand sanitizer became the top commodities. People slowly formed bubbles around themselves as something wrapped in thick-textured plastic. People stayed hidden away behind closed doors. They reminded me of the days when I became invisible, like air, living in a house full of smokers, protecting my lungs, not wanting to cough, gag, sneeze, or smell. However, somehow the internet never disappointed. A man remixed the female rapper, Cardi B saying, "Corona Virus, shit is real!" Its tune went sadly viral. I remembered that dancing and laughter are two necessities to get through anything, and just for a mere second, I would forget about the people with holes in their throats on smoking infomercials—informercials that Dad would utterly frown upon, the mothers and fathers with electronic voices who were the faces of each smoking pamphlet I brought home inside of my backpack. More than anything, I missed Dad more than anyone would ever know.

He would say that they were all full of shit, anyway. And he would express how much he hated the propaganda. Dad's reaction was the same as anti-maskers during the pandemic who believed that wearing a mask is just that: full of shit and more propaganda. I think "shit" was his favorite curse word, and it's probably mine, too—now that I think about it. But, more importantly, Dad would want me to dance and laugh because life is simply too short. "Live your life" was the best advice Dad had given me when I left home. But time was enigmatic—it hasn't been on our side, not in a long time.

LION

I could never get used to the rhythmic sound coming from my dusty alarm clock. Then, the slow, piercing buzz that followed. Not too loud. Not too exhilarating. Not too galling. There was nothing like spending your last dime on a clock sold downrange at the Post Exchange (PX) when deployment money didn't kick in for another thirty days. Those clocks were as basic as they come— black, encased in hollow-like plastic, far from anything special, no radio, no USB port. Basic. All they did was illuminate red numbers barely enough to make them out. But that was enough to get the job done over in Iraq, a place over in the desert that we called the sandbox. A place where the base's lighting was deceiving—the casting rays into the window of our living quarters making it appear that 0200 was really 0700 hours. The thud of my feet hit the ground as I rustled around in the dark, trying to locate my Army physical fitness uniform.

Waking up late was risky. Low crawling with my helmet against the dirt or standing before a superior officer because of ongoing accountability issues was another stressor I did not want or need. I could not add lateness on top of being at war in a foreign country where the air smelled like raw onion and goat cheese from the dining facility. The experience of deploying overseas alone was forever humbling; there was a lack of quality water, lack of sleep, lack of everything.

I returned from my daily duties to a containerized housing unit called a CHU, my temporary home, while living in a war zone in the Middle East. Each CHU was a long white trailer, prefabricated into living quarters. Someone strategically encased green sandbags along the row of CHUs, appearing like green shrubs implanted along with the trailers. The sandbags were each twenty-seven by sixteen inches, made of polypropylene or hessian material stuffed with mounds of sand for flood control, military fortification in trenches and bunkers, or shielding glass windows. A cheap lock cemented the door shut, although it was not secure. A boot to the door will have it flying off the hinges like a bat out of hell. Forget about the restricted view of the mountaintops. The CHU beats living inside a huge tent divided into many compartments with countless other soldiers for several months. I lived in those, too.

You could say the issued keys officially made the CHU a home. Signing the hand receipt for a set of keys felt like signing a lease if you had the creativity to imagine hard enough. If you were born with a silver spoon, you would probably have a tough time imagining the comparison. A short, steel staircase of three or four steps led you up to the only entrance in the CHU. Some called it a stoop; I called it my front porch. A village of CHUs stacked dress right dress or in unison, in a military-styled manner, formed our community within a short walking distance from the area of operation (AO). One way in, one way out.

Many early mornings, I turned my back to the blazing sound coming from the alarm clock until, suddenly, I would hear the voice of a grim reaper coming from the old faithful. There were only so many times you could hit the snooze button after it tells you to wake up quick—Double time! Move!

If I were back home instead of deployed on the other side of the world, I could sleep right through the ringing and buzzing. But while deployed, everything seemed off. After all, I was in another world where decades of war had made a mark on the whole damn country. I tapped the snooze button every day in Iraq. The five minutes added to an eternity, believe it or not. I could get more sound sleep in a matter of minutes than I ever could sleeping eight interrupted hours during most of the night. That's what you can get used to over there—trekking in the sand, broken sleep intervals, the fear of an IED exploding, or taking small arms fire during the middle of the night. I kept my alarm clock close just like my weapon, stationed on the rails of the top metal-framed bunk bed, leaning against the wall.

In the early morning, mid-November rain, a gloom ominously sunk in from the only window in the room. If I were back home in Milwaukee, I would enjoy boot and sweater weather, all those near-naked trees with pieces of their beauty tumbling to the ground. My favorite season—pumpkin spice season, the warming spices of nutmeg, cinnamon, and ginger make me feel warm, safe, cared for, even. Instead, I was surrounded by the overwhelming presence of lifeless trees that never perk up, wild sand, and concrete spaces.

Downrange, when it rained, it poured as if God were angry with us for being in a country that didn't need saving.

I imagined God feeling that type of way. Because it will take a miracle to change anything in that country for the better, something more than man—a miracle that we didn't have packed deep inside of our duffle bags or rucksacks or even stored away inside of our shipping containers. Some of us would discover hard truths later down the road. We'd come face to face with the fates of our marriages, relationships, and family connections; life had simply moved on without us back home.

Sometimes, before I awakened, I could feel what kind of day it would be. Exhausted, I often stared at the ceiling, imagining I could see Orion's Belt, but even that was hard to find on such an ugly, opaque ceiling. Instead, I outlined the shapes of the stars with my fingertips, just like I did many times as a teenager lying flat on a twin bed in an open space in Grandma's attic. Now, boredom frequently visits me. I'd twiddle my fingers and let my hands creep across the wall, realizing that procrastination caused my body to lag far behind.

I never wanted to be late for any of my shifts. But I did not want to report for duty, either, just as I did not want to get up for my shift yesterday. And the day before that. And the week before that. And the month before that. I'd developed a love-hate relationship with my career as a deployed soldier, wondering if the job I was doing ever really mattered at all.

I wondered if I would ever measure up to those Infantry guys. I grew weary, so I stopped thinking about it. I also thought about how changing diapers was something I missed. So much responsibility came with motherhood alone, like selfless service. And being deployed did not make any of my duties lighter. I had a village back home taking care of my responsibilities, making me feel even more guilty and weaker— a mother's sacrifice to leave her children takes a toll.

I am not so sure why my life downrange became monotonous, robotic, even. Each day, I did the same thing: I woke up. I worked out. I conducted personal hygiene. I was in the correct uniform at the right time, on time. I carried my weapon. I sat down at my computer. I looked through my flooded inbox for various personnel action requests that came for processing, prioritizing what was the most important task at hand. I ate chow at the dining facility. I hiked back to the office. I sat down at my computer. I scrolled through more requests that came through while I was gone. I carried my weapon. I ate dinner at the chow hall. I scurried back to the office. I sat down at my computer. I went through more requests that needed processing. Meanwhile, I thought about being away from home for Thanksgiving. I thought about my family waking up Christmas morning when I wouldn't be there opening presents under the tree. Every day, a new thought of missing out. Some days I waited in line at the Morale Welfare and Recreation building (MWR) to get my fifteen-minute phone call home. But the one thing I could bank on every single day was running from explosives going off far too close to the base.

Being downrange, we all looked more mature, almost worn to the core. The smell of Bengay often lingered around the office space. I often wished that it could cure homesickness. I came across a study once that determined that the military ages you. I surfed the internet and discovered it. I don't remember who conducted the study, but the truth of it all became stuck in my head like a bad migraine. Not to mention that female veterans have higher rates of chronic conditions and mental health comorbidities than male veterans or female civilian counterparts. I wondered if this fate was what I had to look forward to once I was done with military service.

One minute you were in civilian clothing taking your photo at the Military Entrance Processing Station, or MEPS, and the next—after four years and a deployment overseas under your belt—you noticed you prematurely developed fine lines and wrinkles. If you stuck around by reenlisting, you often consented to wear and tear on your joints from rucking two or more miles with a load of gear weighing twenty-five pounds or more to prepare yourself for a war you may not ever get to physically see.

Now, when I walk, I can sometimes hear my bones crackling like the sound of an old screen door screeching from the wind—all from before the age of thirty, I tell you. I knew of other jobs in the Army, tougher jobs that will get you down and dirty and often standing on the frontlines. But God did not build me that way. Dad always said I was too girly, always worried about breaking a nail or messing up my hair. Still, working in admin became a nightmare for a gentle soul like mine. I wished Dad could see me now from heaven; I went from having permanent helmet hair that was thinning around the perimeter and won't lie right no matter what gel I used. Now I'm bald.

Anyone who ever processed any type of paperwork or sat behind an office desk knows how mental torture is. The daily destruction of the nervous system: routing mishaps; unchecked boxes; ascertaining proper signatures of authority;

meeting deadlines; paying close attention to detail; flooded email inboxes; multitasking too much; and bottom line, it's a thankless fucking job. But someone had to do it. Because if not, that meant that soldiers standing on the front lines wouldn't get paid, promoted on time, awarded for their dedicated service, evaluated highlighting their annual work performances as soldiers, or even receive care packages sent from loved ones because, in my unit, admin workers controlled the unit's mail as well.

By the end of each day, the load of shitty paperwork creating a mountain on my desk would become replaced by another stack of bullshit, which became even more of a headache to process knowing that the same shit piece of paper had come across my desk multiple times in the past few weeks with the same repeated, egregious errors. By that point, I wanted to scream and pull out my graying hair. The exchange of emails to the sender always seemed to question my competence and my authority as a seasoned Specialist serving in the Army. Besides, although The Department of the Army creates these regulations and pamphlets, nobody reads any of them to know how to do things properly.

Every day in admin, I just knew that I would never be as significant as the Infantry guys down on the front lines because I was sitting on my ass inside of air-conditioned spaces located inside the green or safe zone away from "immediate" danger. I was a fobbit; I never left the forward operating base (FOB) to assist in any heavy lifting. Meanwhile, everybody had an urgent problem that needed to be fixed right at the specific moment and not a second later. But there is only one of me and only so many minutes in one lousy day.

I never really liked who I became downrange. On the outside, I wore the strong face of a lion, a resting bitch face, always on guard and focused on working to make the time go by faster. But, on the inside of my heart, I was missing my family on the other side of the world.

During my downtime, watching movie after movie, purchased from the Local National shops on base downrange for two dollars, made it apparent how my life appeared to me as a black and white rerun series of *The Twilight Zone*. I could describe my deployment experience as a mental state between reality and fantasy with a twisted ending.

The anxiety was exhausting. You would never know when incoming mortar rounds or some type of explosive IED landed somewhere nearby, alerting the sound system. Suddenly, I was calculating when I should shower or even use the bathroom. I worried about being found with my pants down around my ankles, in the squatting position, with my weapon hanging out in the stall's corner within arm's reach. Or, I worried about finding myself stuck in a Porta John, holding my breath from shit baking inside a hole beneath me that was left behind by countless other soldiers, inhaling sewage like secondhand smoke when the loud post command box sounded off, startling me. Incoming. Incoming. Incoming. Seek shelter. Seek shelter. Sirens and countless ammunition rounds popped off, sounding like New Year's Eve or a single night on 27th North Auer Avenue in Milwaukee. Only, I was not celebrating entering a new year. And I was not in the hood. I was in a foreign land where we weren't always welcomed.

My favorite time spent in the Army was occasionally firing my weapon. I loved shooting the pop-up targets more than I enjoyed firing at the paper targets. My best qualifying score placed me as a Sharpshooter—thirty-three out of forty rounds hit the targets.

Jay-Jay often teased me: "At least if I am standing in front of you, I have a good chance of not getting hit."

"As if you were any better," I'd snap back.

"Shiiid! They don't call me Chitty-Chitty Bang-Bang for nuthin." Jay-Jay was a mechanic in the Army. Tasha worked as a supply sergeant. The Army deployed all three of us in Iraq across different parts of the country in one deployment. I think Dad watched CNN every single day while we all were away. I had to tell him to stop watching the news. They don't always report accurate information, or at least not right away. "Someone dressed in Army uniform would show up at your door if anything happened to us," I reassured him. But Dad preferred his news station, anyway. My siblings and I never met up downrange, sadly; the timing was never right. Maybe if we had "admirable" jobs in the Army, that would have been possible. Even though my sister and I always exchanged some-times gossip, quirky letters with hearts, doodles, and emojis, I still felt alone and homesick all the time.

I was a part of The Second Brigade Combat Team be-longing to The First Cavalry Division when we took on an advise and assist role for Operation New Dawn in 2011. The Department of the Army set the deployment to be our last tour in Iraq, leaving behind a historic legacy in the coun-try. Even after seven years of war and over four thousand casualties from the U.S., we ended the combat mission in December of that year.

Former President Barack Obama once said, "In the end, only Iraqis can resolve their differences and police their streets." I wish I could frame that statement. Near the end, we found no evidence of weapons of mass destruction. Instead, we found ourselves in the middle of a lion's den. We found out who we were amid conflict and uncertainty. And all I can think about were the fallen comrades we lost in the unit during the deployment rotation. They were soldiers who came home on a plane in caskets instead of marching with the rest of the unit on the Division's parade field across The First Cavalry Division, followed by live music, mounted troopers on horseback, Stetsons, and spurs, loud cheers, roars, and "welcome home" signs. Their names were read off with no response of "Here, First Sergeant." Their names echoed the sound of silence in the rows of soldiers trying to hold back the tears creeping into the corners of their eyes.

I was a writer long before I ever realized it but in a different capacity. The Army made me one. I learned how to make soldiers seem like they walked on water. I remember typing up a military award citation for another fallen comrade recognizing his sacrifice and service to this nation. But this time was unlike how I had trained and rehearsed countless times over about what to do in the case of a casualty in the unit. I knew this person, not personally, but I recognized his name when his packet came across my desk. Yet, he was given the same five-line citation as if he were just like every other deceased soldier—nothing different than his rank and duty title. I knew that his family would want to read about the soldier he was, what kind of impact he made on his battle buddies, and maybe even the details of how he died, but they wouldn't get that from me. They'd get a dressed-up presentation, a clean version of the soldier's tale. They wouldn't get the dust, dirt, and blood beneath the sand. They wouldn't get the prayers and cries hidden inside military trenches and camouflaged barriers.

With the touch of each key, I felt the weight of each casket being rested on my shoulders. My hands were shaky, almost sensitive to touch. My heart pounded with every keystroke, knowing that messing up this form would mean that the fallen wouldn't lie in their caskets with the proper awards, their uniforms incomplete, and their families not knowing what kind of soldier they truly were in our unit. Each stroke was a burden on my soul, a heaviness in my chest. Their deaths seemed final when I submitted the forms, somehow more real with the reminder that, one day, someone might do this for me.

War is not what you see in movies. It is not a glorified story about an American soldier returning home from war a hero and saving the day. While war is primarily political for most people, for me it's more complicated than that. War for me is working in a support military occupational specialty no one waves a hand about until something goes wrong, somebody doesn't get paid the right entitlement, or somebody's paperwork gets buried beneath a pile of dust. War for me is also waking up to cheap five-dollar alarm clocks purchased at the PX so you won't be late to first formation in the morning. War is all the return-without-action emails sent to units due to jacked-up paperwork constantly coming across your desk just in time for the sirens to broadcast Seek shelter, Incoming. War is casualty notifications and award citations for a fellow soldier who met their end in yesterday's IED attack. War is polishing a weapon you never get to fire but sprinting to take cover during a real firestorm. It's worrying if you're going to get killed while trying to take a dump in a Porta John. It's waking up every day knowing that your last one might be today, or at the very least, tomorrow. It's missing out on your baby's first footsteps, holiday meals with family, unwrapping gifts under the tree, and your third wedding anniversary. It's coming home feeling like a stranger in your own home because life went on without you. War is having your family look at you weird at family reunions, hearing from them how you've changed, and how you think you are better than everyone else because you ran off to the Army. War is also saving deployment money because there is nowhere to spend it all and returning home hoping to become debt-free, to give your children most things you never had and more.

Specifically, war is the back of my neck taking a strong beating from the blazing heat beaming down on Warhorse. Sal, my M-16, slung loosely against my back. I felt a cool drizzle tread lightly down the curvature of my spine. It tickled a little, the itch I couldn't scratch. I tried to ignore it by relaxing my mind, so I called cadence to myself—left-right, left.

On this day, my hands were full of Army green award binders. Two other soldiers walked along beside me. One was my supervisor, Sergeant First Class Jackson, a real stickler for attention to detail and redlining paperwork, and the other Specialist; we were battle buddies before I pinned Sergeant. A battle buddy is someone who would never leave a fallen comrade. My battle buddy, Specialist Tisdale, shared my same fear; she never wanted to be caught in a Porta John or latrine while the enemy hit the FOB with indirect fire. So, we scheduled our bathroom visits at the same time daily after chow at 1400. It was better to be safe than sorry.

We headed down the path to the company's headquarters about 200 meters away. The birds had long gone from the sky. For the first time during the deployment, the sky appeared empty and colorless. The trees turned ominously dark. The air smelled of spoiled milk. Local Nationals working on the base packed up their bodegas, closing their small shops all at the same time and much earlier than normal. We didn't make it twenty-five meters before the loud explosion came without warning. The first big bang alerted the giant command voice box to blast. Incoming. Incoming. Incoming. Seek shelter. Seek shelter. Seek shelter. The impact rattled the ground. Rocks and debris flung violently in the air. My ears went mute. I felt the ground beneath my feet become unstable.

The reign of a three-headed dragon destroyed our route to safety, ready to throw flames from its mouth and set us ablaze with its venomous breath. We took the path of least resistance, locating the only bunker within fifty meters of open space and rubble. The rising smoke obscured our surroundings with charcoal grays. With little to no visibility, all we could do was stay low and move with a sense of urgency. The rocks no longer made the same crunching sound as they did when we rucked the way to the headquarters. Instead, the sounds were piercing as the rocks launched mid-air among the shower of mortar rounds.

The sounds of battle had begun. My battle buddy SPC Tisdale took off and left SFC Jackson and me. She yelled, "Come on!" But her accent did not allow her to say "on." She had a slight twang, dragging "on" like come "moan." My soul departed; my legs lagged. Somewhere in between me slowly catching up to my feet, I lost my head cover. My patrol cap flew in the opposite direction as if it had a mind of its own. Dodging dancing rocks to retrieve it, I didn't remember the rules of engagement; I only remembered accountability, maintaining my equipment, and presentation of self—presentation of my uniform.

I was in the best shape of my life but panting heavily. SFC Jackson double-timed as he zoomed ahead of me. He scolded me from afar, screaming at me, shouting at me to bring my ass on and to hurry up as he made it to the concrete bunker where SPC Tisdale hid. They were so fast; I was not. I had never noticed the bunker within fifty meters up ahead. My body tried to not die.

Hiding in the bunker, I thought about what Dad would do in the same scenario. He was a lion. He'd buddy carry me through the chaos of madness and into the serenity of safety.

"You a'right?" Staff Sergeant Tillman asked from the other end of the bunker. "I'm surprised you still got those awards planted in your hand. I would have let that shit go. Are you sure you a'right? I couldn't speak. "You good?" Staff Sergeant Tillman revealed his pearly whites.

"Yes." I could only whisper. But I lied. I was not. I was really not good. I held my head low, my heart feeling like it was about to rip out of my chest. The baked salmon I ate made its way settling in the pit of my throat. I wanted to hurl but couldn't.

"You are really dedicated," SPC Martinez said. He laughed to himself and then towards SSG Tillman. "She still got them damn awards, man." My reaction never wavered. I was still afraid. I thought about any last wishes until I heard SPC Martinez speak again: "She will never leave a fallen award." Several others chuckled.

Great. I'm soup-sandwich. Look at me. I'm a mess. I'm a joke. I stared down at my un-bloused boots, my shoelaces undone. I counted the sounds of the blast—twenty booms. Then, I lost count. Hearing twenty booms was just like hearing a thousand.

Every soldier had a different military occupational specialty, a different assigned duty for that day, and a different reaction to what seemed to be a never-ending blast. What brought us together was the most intense and terrifying experience some of us will ever encounter, not only in our military careers but in our entire lives. Although we were above ground, we were in a void of darkness, as if we were soon to be buried deep amongst the debris, the rubble, the smoke.

I never realized that, tightly wedged into my chest, were the Army green award binders I still held in my arms. I never made it up the road to the company's headquarters to distribute the awards for the later presentation. After the initial blast, I thought I had thrown them in the air. But there they were, intact in my arms like I'd been comforting a small child. I held on to those binders; that was my fight. They were all I knew.

Throughout the bunker were sniffles, racing hearts, excessive sweating, and silent cries. I hoped. I wished. And I prayed, but my prayer was rather selfish than selfless:

In God I trust, but I am still afraid. At this point in my life, I am asking for mercy. Please God… if this is my last day on Earth, I am almost certain that I am not ready to go just yet. There are so many things… things that I didn't get to complete. I want to see my kids grow up. I want to hug my dad again. I want to graduate from college. I do not want such a poor photo from Basic Training plastered on an obituary or on CNN News. Please God...it's such a horrible picture. If you spare my life, I promise I will go to church every Sunday – Amen.

Many mortars made it over the barriers. Then, complete silence. Finally, after several minutes, security forces alerted us with the all-clear. Being held up inside the bunker felt like an eternity. All I knew was that I had clung to those binders and the false sense of hope that this day would never happen to me, but it did. I did not know what to expect on my way out of the bunker or why I was so surprised the blasts did as much damage as they did. The mortars took out everything behind our headquarters building; the wreckage had landed everywhere. I glanced up at the roof of the bunker and thanked God that it stayed.

The dry heat howled like some horror movie opener and the sky was dark as night. But when I managed to focus on my watch, it was almost 1500 hrs. The sweat drizzled violently down the sides of my face I could barely find my way back inside the headquarters. After accounting for everyone and traveling down to the aid station to get checked out, I phoned home, not to repeat what just occurred, but to hear the voices of the people I loved.

We didn't lose any lives that day, but there were some injuries, injuries that many civilians can't see through the smiles: the nightmares, the anxieties, the flashbacks, the self-isolation, the feeling as though trapped inside a maze you can't escape. I evaluated whether military life was for me. I evaluated the relevance of a paper-pushing desk job in Iraq. I signed up for one thing and got another. The truth is, everybody wants to be a lion until it is time to do some lion kind of shit.

I wish I was as brave as SSG Tillman who'd asked me if I was okay in the bunker. I wish I could laugh in the face of danger. He must have hauled ass from one hundred meters instead of fifty to make it safely inside. He carried an M9 holstered around his right thigh, instead of a musket like I did. I bet he was Infantry. As he leaned forward to catch his breath, he'd braced both knees before he glanced up at me. He did not budge as the rounds landed around the outside of the barrier, as if what we were experiencing was another training exercise. He didn't panic. He didn't break a sweat. He didn't obviously pray. Instead, he tried to lighten the mood.

I fantasized about the ferociousness of a fearless lion like a father. While I silently cried at the thought of unexpected death, I wished that I could pinch myself and realize that it was all a dream where I could wake up to the cringing sound of a cheap five-dollar alarm clock. I wished that I would have never gone back to retrieve a patrol cap of all unnecessary things. I wished that I would have thrown every award into the air so that they could burn. But it didn't matter. It didn't matter because I would be typing hundreds more for the commander to present to all the men and women who were under attack and in immediate danger from the insurgents. This time, I would be among the special pile of award citations not given to the Infantry – the Combat Action Badge. I would don a rectangular shield supporting both an M9 bayonet and an M67 grenade wrapped with an oak wreath across my right side just parallel to my waistline. I felt unworthy of such an award because I didn't do anything brave. I just managed to stay alert and stay alive.

I wished the summer of 2011 wouldn't have affected me as much as it did. If only I were a lion, like him.

SANDY, RANDY & CANDY

Every journey starts at home. That's what I told myself when I decided to give one more shot at interviewing Mama about her family. Things were different this time; after all, I was an adult, she lived in my home, and I was a mother now, too. I needed her help with tending to my children while I played Captain Marvel. I guess you could say that I got desperate. I figured I should make amends with Mama and the role she played in my life.

I collected my saliva and sent it off to be tested. I thought I deserved to know the truth, the real reason why she was taken away at birth to foster care. I deserved to know why she always had the fear of being alone. I deserved to know why she has become so dependent on me and my family and why somehow our roles as parent and child were reversed. I deserved to know why I have been obsessed with the idea of being a "good" mom to my own children for as long as I can remember.

Mama sat quietly in her usual chair at the rounded glass table in my living room. The sunlight beamed through lace curtains hanging from a large patio door behind her. She was skimming through the pages of her Bible that had busted at the seams. I pulled up a chair across from her. Steve Harvey's voice echoed in the background amidst soft laughter on *Family Feud*, but I managed to stay focused.

I shared with Mama the process of submitting my DNA to find some of her living relatives with the hopes of learning more about her biological parents and I also got the results back. She pretended to be happy for me. Her smile seemed forced as her large body tensed up in her chair. The energy I was looking for just simply wasn't there.

"I know there may be family secrets revealed, and I'm prepared for that," I said. She looked down at her Bible and then back up at me. I think this time, it was real for her as it was real for me; she knew I meant business. I pulled up the app on my phone that displayed our heritage in a full-color pie chart. I continued to be delighted at the moment because the moment was mine. I showed her:

"See, I'm thirty-five percent Nigerian, twenty percent Cameroonian, eleven percent Irish, ten percent Malian, nine percent Ghanian. The Irish ancestry I know is from Dad. Grandma Lizz said so." Mama looked enigmatically into my phone screen.

"Did this cost you a lot of money?"

"No. That's not important."

"Oh."

"What's important," I said, "is what I found in my search."

"And what's that?"

"Here, I printed a news article for you to keep in your Bible. But I thought you said our granddad's name was Herman?" I asked.

The small righthand corner of a section of the Appleton Post Crescent, dated August 1962, listed the birth announcement of newborn triplets:

The 24-year-old wife of an unemployed man gives birth Monday to triplets—their 9th, 10th, and 11th children. A boy and two girls were born to Irma Washington, whose husband, Henry, 30, is on relief. Their other children are Diane, 9; Thomas, 8; 5-year-old twins Ernest and Ernestine; Curtis, 4; Sherman, 3; Herman, 2, Philip, 1, and last, a daughter who would have been 6 died in 1960.

Sitting there in her graphic t-shirt that showcased #1 Mom stretched across her broad chest—the shirt she purchased herself at Walmart—she finally gave me the reaction I was hoping for. That response was appreciation, and even joy although the hospital put the wrong name on the announcement. Herman was written on Mama's birth certificate. I asked her if the names of her siblings also listed on the announcement were familiar to her. She acknowledged they were. At that moment, she revealed to me the best she could of what she knew from her life before.

Mama and her siblings were young when they were taken. She struggled to remember her previous life, a life that seemed very foreign to me. Mama sometimes recalled summer days spent playing in the park, swinging high and kicking up dust as her feet scampered along unbeaten terrain. She'd gaze up into the blue sky and through the clouds, hoping to connect to her life from before. She remembered little about her mother, only that she was kind. She was nurturing.

She loved her husband so much that she ran the streets after him, the drunk that he was. But she loved him. She loved Herman so much that she left her babies home alone inside of dresser drawers so she could go bring him home.

Only, Grandpa Herman wasn't as kind and gentle as Grandpa Irma. He seemed crazy at times, especially when he drank away all his earnings, and he never brought food back to feed the family. But she loved him regardless. Maybe love is blind. Maybe not. Maybe love is stupid. Mama and all her siblings were just like me, completely reliant on their parents, only they weren't there; there was no love. For that, I empathize with Mama.

Mama called one of the other triplets over the phone, my Aunt Veronica, while I remained connected to their conversation like a friendly fly on the wall. I knew Aunt Veronica well. Mama and she were close. Unlike Mama, Aunt Veronica gave us eccentric gifts for Christmas. One year, I remember the Christmas snow globe necklace Aunt Veronica was proud to hang around our necks. We shook the globe and watch the snow fall around Santa and his reindeer.

As I listened in on their conversation, it started off pleasant, then it took a turn when Mama revealed to Aunt Veronica my intentions to find our family. "I don't wanna know dem people," said Aunt Veronica. "I wish I never found out about our mother. I would have been better off. I shouldn't have ever listened to my friend when she said that she could help us find out where our mother was. She said she knew how to locate our mother using a phone book to look up every Washington and call them to ask if they had triplets, two girls, and a boy. I regret I ever went. I was happy where I was. I was smart. I had good grades. I wanted to be a lawyer. I could have made something of myself. Instead, I went to find our mother, and I ended up being abused. I got abused. I was on the streets. My life changed. I had no one to take me in. You had people who took you in. You. Ronald. I didn't have anybody who loved me. I finally have somebody who loves me, my husband, and he takes care of me. So, no. No thank you, I don't wanna know. I don't wanna know dem people. And you shouldn't wanna either, just leave it alone."

Mama said, "Veronica, you sound like you are blaming me. It's not my fault. Our foster mother treated me bad. She treated you and Ronald good, but she beat the hell out of me. I was left-handed. She said I was evil and made me write with my right hand. Every time I would pick the pencil up to write with my left hand, she'd beat my ass. You were the smart one. I was not. I brought home D's. Every time I brought in bad grades, that woman would beat me… Tisha wants to find out who our family is. She gave her DNA and is searching on Ancestry. She is asking me questions. I don't know what else to tell her. When we found our mother by looking her up in the phonebook, we called every Washington in the phone book and when we finally found her, she answered the phone and screamed and said my babies found me, and then we asked her can we stay with her, she said yes, and when we ran away from our foster mom to go be with her, she died. We went to another foster home. We were together, me and you. Ronald went to a different home, and then you, Veronica, you left me. You ran away to go stay with our older sister, Ernestine. You chose to stay with them. It's not my fault."

At this point, I had to interject. "Hi, Auntie," I said, "My mama is right. I wanted to know who our family is." I needed to know for myself and my children. I needed to know what mental illnesses and other health issues run in the family. I needed to know so my children don't end up marrying their cousins.

"If I were you, I would leave it alone," Aunt Veronica said.

We ended the call. I asked Mama what her problem was. Mama said Ernestine wasn't very kind to her. She had her out on the streets making fast money. I felt so sorry for Aunt Veronica, so sorry she couldn't be the lawyer she wanted to be. She didn't deserve that life; neither of them did.

At this point, Mama began to rock back and forth in her chair. She said that it was best that Aunt Veronica get it all out, release all the anger, and pray about it. Then she threw up her hands, looking away from me. And that was the moment I realized that Mama and her siblings were truly broken people who needed to be loved. I ended the day by deciding that it was best not to say anything else to her about my quest to find my family.

The next morning, I walked downstairs to the kitchen for coffee, and I overheard Mama talking on the phone in the next room. Amazingly, it sounded like she'd found more long-lost family. She called me over and introduced me to Thelma. I wondered how long she'd known about Thelma, an ex who was married into Mama's side of the family. She'd married Grandma Irma's brother Jewel. Thelma knew Irma well when she also stayed over on Capitol Drive, three streets over from Grandma Lizz and Grandpa Zeke Sr.

Thelma would then put me in contact with a long-lost uncle, Grandma Irma's younger brother, Uncle Walter. Uncle

Walter was just sixteen years old when he made the trip up to Milwaukee from Louisiana, the last time he saw his older sister. The first time I heard my Uncle Walter's euphonious voice over the phone, I had thrilled ears. He was a very articulate man with a radio voice, and, remarkably, he revealed that he'd always been wondering about us and looking for us, too. When I asked him about my Grandma Irma, I didn't want to miss any details of his account. The way he spoke about her gave me chills.

Speaking to Walter thrilled the hell out of me. I never knew I would get as far as I did with my genealogy. I supposed, eight years of college education paid off. Uncle Walter answered my call delighted to speak with me. Turned out he'd been searching for us too. I let him know that I received his phone number from Thelma. Irma Brown was Uncle Walter's older sister.

I felt like I needed a pen and pad to write down everything Uncle Walter had to share. In fact, I was surprised that he didn't know my grandfather Herman; he only heard of him. Uncle Walter apologized for not being able to provide any information on Herman but offered to make a few phone calls and get back to me. I admired how thoughtful Uncle Walter was and appreciated his grace. He said he always wondered what happened to all those kids Irma had when she died.

Herman's father, Walter Brown Sr. was married to his first wife, Annie Lester Jackson who was Irma's mother. They divorced. He got with Uncle Walter's mother, Idell Grant. They separated. Then after Uncle Walter's mother, he married Irene Green. Walter helped me with a list of siblings that Irma had. Because I would probably never get the opportunity to meet some of them, I felt empowered to list their names, to know they were real:

Jewel Brown, the oldest brother married to Thelma; Eloy Grant, we called him Syrup; Dee Bullock, of Oak Ridge, Louisiana; Ardis Green, Los Angeles, California; Andrew Johnson, we call him AJ, Dallas, Texas; James Bullock, Shreveport, Louisiana; Walter Shine, California about eighty miles from San Francisco, Johnny Ray, Uncle Walter's half-brother from Irene Green, Dallas, Texas; Annie Pearl Bullock and Rebecca Brown, Acadia, Louisiana; Joann Brown, Bobby Brown, Annie Hill, and Lois Jean Green, Dallas, Texas, Flora Johnson, Oak Ridge, Louisiana; Lora Johnson, Oakland, California; Lois C. Green, Monroe, Louisiana, and Ola Marshal, Los Angeles, California.

I spent a lot of time catching up with Uncle Walter. I wanted to know what Irma looked like. Did she look like me? I wanted to know what she was like as a person. Was she like Mama? Irma's personal life appeared to be more of a mystery to even Uncle Walter.

"Irma would come down to visit but she never talked about her life," he said. "She would come down alone. She suffered in silence you know. I was sixteen years old the last time I saw her," Uncle Walter said.

"Is it true she was mentally ill?" I asked. "She had all those babies. And is that why they were all taken away?" I was afraid I asked. I was afraid to offend Uncle Walter.

"Well, she had some problems," Uncle Walter suggested. But I was itching to know more details. I hoped Walter didn't get too shy with me about Irma.

"I heard she jumped in the Milwaukee River. Is this true?" I asked. I could hear him sigh over the phone. I took a deep breath and braced myself for his response.

"Yes, that did happen. She was institutionalized right after for a few months. I visited her while she was in the hospital. She walked out to greet me; she was like a ten-year-old—broken. She was a big woman five foot eleven, over three hundred pounds...having all those kids, an alcoholic husband...when I saw her, she was at her worst, but you know what? She loved you guys very much. Thelma Jean, Jewel's ex-wife, said that Irma was the sweetest woman with a good heart. She was a good person...she didn't deserve the abuse. Life just took her out. She didn't get any relief. Herman got with her at fourteen years old...you know when I was a kid, she took care of me. She nicknamed me Boogie."

"Boogie, that's cute. I wish I could have met her," I said. I wished I was given a nickname. I sat there, shoulders hunched and a stiff neck. I thought about how special Uncle Walter must be to have a nickname.

"Yeah...it wasn't long after the visit to Milwaukee that she passed away."

"Well, I was able to order an uncertified copy of Grandma Irma's death certificate. It said she died at thirty-nine years old in 1976 of arteriosclerotic heart disease." I could hear the crack in my voice. I cleared my throat and repositioned myself onto the chair.

"That sounds about right, kiddo. She had a lot of health issues. I was sixteen years old in 1976 when we visited and then months later came back for her funeral."

When I ordered Grandma Irma's death certificate, as well as her birth certificate, I wanted a small piece of her that I never had. I never realized that having two pieces of paper would open this new world to me. I wondered why Grandma Irma chose to marry Herman. I wondered if she really had a choice. I wondered why Herman chose alcohol over his wife and kids. At least there was one thing Mama was good at—she was really good at choosing my dad. He took care of his family. He was our rock. Talking to Uncle Walter on the phone made me miss talking to Dad.

"Tell me more about you, Uncle Walter," I said. "What brought you out to California from Louisiana?"

"Well... I was the black sheep of the family...I didn't really fit in. I was a Navy guy. I spent three and a half years in the Navy Honor Guard in Washington, D.C. I don't have a prison record. It's crazy in a way... but it's life...I lived long enough to know that people make their own choices. Whatever the addiction is, they become trapped...I was very fortunate to go on another path. I was looking for you guys four years ago."

"I'm glad I found you. I am a veteran, too. Army. I medically retired early...served only ten years...been deployed to Iraq and Afghanistan...my brother Jay-Jay and my sister Tasha are both Army veterans as well and both been to the sandbox."

"Take down my email address. I want to share a story about your grandmother later. You should also probably take down Barry's number. Barry and your grandmother were very close. Barry is Thelma and Jewel Brown's son. He was also Irma's favorite nephew. But I must warn you, Barry's a talker."

"Okay. That's fine. I don't mind if that means I get more information about my grandmother. Thank you, Uncle Walter. I'll talk to you soon."

I told Mama what Uncle Walter said—that he had been looking for us for four years, he wondered what happened to us, all the names he was able to spew out at me at the drop of a dime, and what he remembered of her mother Irma. She smiled. I handed Mama Uncle Walter's phone number so that she could also keep in touch with him, too.

It took me a couple months to reach out to Barry. I think I needed a pause, to take everything in, to process all the information that I discovered about my family. I didn't want to psych myself out. I thought about what Barry may think about me calling him after all this time. Would he even want to hear from me? He may think that I am just another crazy member of the family he didn't want to know like Auntie Veronica. Maybe he would be traumatized like her. I didn't know. I just knew I came too far to walk away now. The worst he could say is no, I don't wanna know dem people. But I hoped. I hoped Barry would embrace me as Uncle Walter did.

One day, I finally made the call. "Hello Barry," I said when he picked up. "My name is Tisha. I got your number from Walter. I was reaching out to you because I wanted to know more about Irma Brown. She was my grandmother. She had a set of triplets. One of her triplet girls is my mama, Virginia. If you have some free time, I would love to ask you some questions."

"Hey, little cuz. Irma Brown was my auntie. She was the nicest person you would ever meet."

"I heard from Uncle Walter that you were her favorite."

"Yeah…I dunno why. I guess because I was the first son. I was a little kid when I met Irma. Right. No one could pick with me around her. She just called me her favorite. I did not mind as long as I got treats. Right."

"Do you have any pictures with her?"

"No. And I don't know why I don't have pictures. I was also close to her sister Auntie Annie Pearl. She passed away in 2013. Right. I went to Arcadia, Louisiana to her funeral. I always wanted to know about the family. Right. Auntie Annie Pearl would say, you don't have to worry about them, they can't hurt you no more baby. I always wondered what she meant by that. Right. I just wanted to know about them. Are they bad folks? Are they outlaws or sumthin'?"

"I heard not-so-good things about the family. I heard bad things about both my grandma and grandpa. Did you know my grandpa Herman?"

"I knew him as Cheffy. I didn't know Herman. He loved to drink. Right. Every now and then she would have spousal problems. She had trouble existing. She was having babies left and right. I remember she had given birth to one of her babies early in the morning and went to work that evening. Cheffy was a drunk. But she was a big woman. Right. She could handle herself if she wanted to. One time I seen her push Cheffy, and the whole house shook."

"Did you know anything about her jumping into the Milwaukee River?"

"When I was in the fifth or sixth grade, I remember we had a class assignment where we had to share current events about what we had seen in the news. Right. One of the other kids in my class brought in an article about a lady that jumped in the Milwaukee Harbor because God told her to do it. He read her name to the class. I didn't want to say in the class that, that was my auntie. Right."

"Yeah, I get why you would be ashamed to say something. I didn't know she was religious."

"Auntie was really religious. She baptized me in the bathroom sink. Right. She said do you love Jesus? I said yes, I love Jesus. You shall be saved. Then she started splashing water on me from the sink. I was like six or seven years old. Right. I wasn't judgmental. Even as a little kid, I tried to understand. Right. She was a gentle giant."

"How old are you, Barry? You sound so young?"

"I was born in 1960."

"My mama was born in 1962. Have you ever seen any of Irma's kids?"

"I saw some of them, but not all of them."

"I just hear how she was so good to you and how you have good memories of her, her children, they didn't have those same memories that you have."

"I dunno, little cuz. She was struggling to feed them. She couldn't afford it. Right. Uncle Cheffy spent all the money any way he wanted to."

Barry and I talked for over an hour about Irma, her sister Annie Pearl, and the rest of the demented family. Many of them were scary people. Many of them I will never meet in person. Many of them are no longer living; they died off too soon from freak accidents like being electrocuted while talking outside on the pay phone, being hit by a tractor-trailer truck, and from health issues ranging from alcoholism to heart issues and poor eating habits. It's unfortunate that Mama and I wasted so much time dancing around the hard truths. And the truth is that none of the visions I previously held was my perfect family, The Huxtables, or my perfect home with white vinyl siding, large bay windows, and black shutters, featuring that red door and white picket fence—none of this was my reality. I was a little girl lost in a dream full of strangers; I tried to fill some indescribable void with anything I could instead of accepting that fact. And the truth is, for the first time, I felt woke.

Growing up, my only wish was that my life was all a dream and, when I'd awaken, I'd be Rudy Huxtable. I really wanted to search for the truth in my family, the truth in me. And now, I really wanted to tell a fantasy where I grew up in a rough neighborhood, made it out, started a perfect family, joined the Army, and went to war, then came home a hero.

I couldn't.

I never wanted to make my family look bad. I wanted to tell a fantasy, and change every name to Cliff, Claire, Vanessa, Theo, Denise, Cassandra, Alvin, and Olivia. I wrote it. Then, I ripped it into tiny shreds. It would have been the fantasy that everyone would want to read, but, instead, I decided to write my truth.

A LETTER TO A YOUNG DAD

I knew you. Before I was born, in the form of an angel, I knew you. I knew the alto of your voice. The joy of your laugh. And the greatest hits you played from 8 tracks to vinyl records to cassette tapes—Rapper's Delight, LL Cool J, Run DMC—with me riding around in the back seat of an all-white Cadillac with the emblem sitting pretty in the front. The car was almost whistle clean, except on one side where there was one rust spot near the back left tire. You liked your seat laid back with the windows down and one hand gripping the stirring wheel. The smoke from your Newport created a halo around your head, so you held your cigarette out of the window, out in the air like passing a torch. The same torch my future brother and sister would take on, that bad habit of smoking. But not me, says the blind man — you're the reason I am who I am today. Wise. Headstrong. The reason I'm still holding on.

The year was 1980 when black fathers had names like Tyrone and Mike and Curtis and carried bottles of Crown Royal in their back pockets. You were Him. You were Zeke. You were my dad. And when I'm born soon, I will grow to love you more than the world could ever know. Until I'm much older, I will know you from old pictures. My favorite is the one of you and me. You're wearing Levi's jeans. You're sitting on the front stoop of a house. You're holding the newborn me next to a young girl adding clean crisp cornrows to another's afro hair. It would be the first time I would hear the song you made just for me—a cheesy song, a song about how you are the greatest dad. I cooed and smiled, not wanting the song to ever end, never realizing that there will be a time when the song would abruptly end, and I will forever mourn madly.

I was small like a doll with my mother's hair and the silhouette of your face. As I grew, we'd have the same bow leg, swiveled side tooth, and crooked smile. We'd even laugh at the same movies, the same jokes, the same everything. We'd be inseparable until the end.

I also knew you from the way that you lit up every room with the sound of your laugh. I have your presence. "You look just like your damn daddy," Mama would say. She was just jealous, Daddy. You were so fine. You aged like wine. Your words held power even when your voice was very faint – the sound of how echoes plummet. Even now, I feel you with me as cogently as the smoke rising from your Newport cigarettes. When I move, we are one. I follow your footsteps until they've gone cold and fade to nothing more than your lingering scent.

You're long gone. Since 2019, I have never been the same. I can still smell the smoke mixed with Cool Water cologne and fresh Pine Sol. I can still hear your footsteps sweeping, then mopping, across the hardwood floor early Sunday mornings. You cleaned to Al Green, Frankie, Beverly, Maze, and the Isley Brothers, too. I can still feel the high pitch in your voice when it cracked a million times, slapping my eardrums when you were trying to imitate Al.

I miss you, Dad. I miss your sound. As I hold back tears, I hope we will one day meet again in a different world, a different life. I hope that when we see one another again we will meet to Al's song, the song we played for you on your death bed, and the song we played for you at your homegoing— "Love and Happiness."

They say that red birds symbolize a happy sign that those we have lost will live forever so long as we keep their memory alive in our hearts. They generally appear when you need or miss them the most. I know because you send red birds whenever I'm feeling blue.

I wish life were a magic trick. Alakazam. I wish life were like a fairy tale, once upon a time not long ago. Or life as a fictional creation, somewhere off in a galaxy far, far away. I wish life were a stage play or a musical, just easing on down the yellow brick road. I wish life were a piece of cake. But it's not. And I'm living in another world without you.

Life is staring out the wide window, wondering what's it like wherever you are. Wondering if I will ever see you again, or if you're a ghost or spirit or my guardian angel. Or, perhaps, wondering if you are now a butterfly passing through each life cycle. Life is playing our songs on repeat. Life is becoming you when responding to my chatty, clingy children. "Mom, can we have McDonald's?" They often beg. And I'll respond, "You got McDonald's money?" They won't ask again because the answer means no. And, what am I? "Do I look like I'm made out of money?" I'll forever hold on to all my myriad of magnificent memories and visions of you.

In the end, that's all I have left. The lingering smell of Cool Water cologne. Pine Sol spread across hardwood floors. A pack of Newport's, the menthol kind. A cold Pepsi and a nice smile. I see visions of you standing in the doorway whenever there's trouble. "Don't mess around and write a check that your ass can't cash."

We had a good run, you, and me. I will be forever thankful that, I knew you.

A NOTE TO MY MOM

Ijust want you to know…Mommy, Mom, Irma, my beautiful mom whom I'll always love because you gave me life. I thank God for you because I am a gift from God. Only God could determine my birth and predestine my life, so I have no regrets. No matter how my life turns out, I promise to be the woman of God I'm destined to be. I know you're proud of me. It's a comfort know you're in heaven and you can know God's in control and has me in his hands and I'm loved by friends and family far and near. I love you always.

Virginia (Sandy)

EPILOGUE

Mama's gone. Aunt Veronica drove down I-90 East and got her. They deserve each other and I mean that with all due respect. I could no longer take on her high blood pressure, seizures, and dramatic antics. I once felt that a nursing home would be best. Now, I would never know. I do know early mornings are the best.

I awaken to a fleet of oak trees surrounding a condo I own in central Virginia and no longer stress. I stand on my back deck and observe the sun coating the treetops with the luster of goldmines. I often reflect in the same place, in the same stance, in my special place on the deck. A large natural wood deck, that elegantly wraps around my unit, is where I realize that these specific trees are the very same thick-barked, acorn-baring trees that withstood every hurricane that shook the city. The same fine oak trees are now flourishing, looking back at me, solid and strong as if they were reincarnated from palm trees in another life. I only knew of palm trees that typically bend in gusty weather with ease, without losing their pineapple-like beauty, but not my trees. They are built differently. They are from humble beginnings. Fighters.

Something that surprises me about my backyard is that the heart of every oak tree still beats. Their roots run rampant, although they have experienced a catastrophe. Despite the empty gaps, where part of the branches once reigned, they stand not tall, but C-shaped, bowed. They've been carrying the weight of the world on their shoulders, yet they still bear leaves. I wonder, why can't people be more like trees?

Oh, it's a remarkable thing to see my trees bowing at the knees, fatigued but functioning, bending but not breaking, as they continue to rise through every occasion, even through stormy weather. I know that they stood their ground at the end of the road, even if the force of nature wreaked havoc all around them, destroying powerlines, causing major power outages, flooding, and other damage from heavy winds and rain.

I also know that my relationship with family has formed me just like those trees—bending but not breaking. I never got that apology; you know, a true apology that I expected from Mama for staying in a relationship with Dave, for forcing me to be a part of the world he tried to create for me where he dominated, and I stayed afraid. Instead, I got the response of I gave you away to your dad to protect you, so you didn't have to see me abused. See her, abused? What about the little girl, me? I thought about how I would thank her and tell her how lucky I was that she gave birth to me, that she didn't throw me away in the streets. I thought about how I am lucky because, if it weren't for her, I wouldn't have my dad. I thought about how everything I am and everything that I've hoped to become all began with her. I thought about how I love her, still, through every violent word that stemmed from the sweetest smile I've ever seen. I thought about how much-hurt people hurt people, and yes, it really, really, really sucks.

All that is left of Mama is a rendition of her childhood written in a red composition notebook she kept as a journal. I found it tucked away in a box of her belongings she left behind. It began with, "Couldn't call mother, MOTHER." Her foster mother told her that they were placed with her instead of placed in a circus without any other details. Sandy, Randy, and Candy were born with birth defects in both legs and feet which were broken and fitted for casts in hopes of straight feet. They wore brown leather combat boots with steel bars along the side of the boots. Eventually Sandy grew severe bunions on both toes from years of wearing shoes that were way too small. Sandy was Mama's old name. She had the perfect pair of knock-knees to match her bunions. Sandy had a bad habit of sucking her fingers and she'd bump her head against her bed to go to sleep at night. Sandy's journal also noted:

> I had trouble in school. Because I never was good at Math. I always had to write my multiplication facts from zero to twelve. And spelling tests were hard for me too. Going to Locust Street Library was my tutoring. After being chased home daily and made to fight, me having to watch my sister Veronica fight, don't know why girls didn't like her or wanted to fight her. But one day in particular, my sister was chased home from Fulton Middle School. She fought this girl, and I remembered her friend Barbara who lived down the street from us would

help keep the fights fair by not letting all the girls jump her. But me, I cried. I wouldn't help her fight cause I was shy and didn't know why all the girls – My sister wasn't scared though. She beat this one girl bad though. They fought all the way to 3029 North 5th Street, where we lived, and she ran into the house. Mrs. Butler, made us go back outside and fight, even me. If we didn't get that mob away from our house, we were going to get beat and we did anyway for running from a fight.

Eventually, I will burn the journal. It will no longer be my burden to carry. I will awaken each day staring at the largest oak tree nearby. It's the tree I see when walking out of my sliding door. It's a peculiar tree; somewhere along the way, the trunk split in two. The tree could easily fall over onto my unit, destroying my home, but it won't. It has survived every hurricane season since 2015. And, after a while, I noticed that the opening in the tree is now a natural habitat, a jungle gym for squirrels and possums to hide and seek.

What I've learned through living my life and building these intricate relationships with family is that life doesn't always mirror a perfectly-shaped oak tree. And sometimes trauma, grief, and even pain look like a fleet of oak trees bending at the knees surrounding a condo located in central Virginia. The point is, I will survive. I will forgive. And, just like the trees, I won't forget. Mama would never forget. Although she may waddle in her shame. I'm sure she felt guilty. That's why it is so easy for her to be distant, and with her sister in Milwaukee. And, I would never have to wither in her misery. Instead, I'll flourish with the seasons. I know from the spirit world that I'm never alone. Memories of Dad will aid me in my quest for finding joy in the little things. My children will receive a better version of my mother, a better version of me. I will bend, and bow, but not break in my truth and be set free.

Milton Keynes UK
Ingram Content Group UK Ltd.
UKHW040639150923
428743UK00004B/261